CRIME SCENE INVESTIGATIONS

REAL-LIFE SCIENCE LABS
for Grades 6–12

PAM WALKER ♦ ELAINE WOOD

Illustrations by Christopher Stone

**THE CENTER FOR APPLIED
RESEARCH IN EDUCATION**
West Nyack, New York 10994

Library of Congress Cataloging-in-Publication Data

Walker, Pam.
    Crime scene investigations : real-life science labs for grades 6–12 /
  Pam Walker and Elaine Wood : illustrations by Christopher Stone.
        p.   cm.
    ISBN 0–87628–135–8
    1. Science—Study and teaching (Elementary)—Activity programs.
  2. Science—Study and teaching (Secondary)—Activity programs.
  3. Critical thinking—Study and teaching.   I. Wood, Elaine.
    II. Title.
  LB1585.W245   1998
  507.1—dc21   98–14891
                                                                  CIP

Illustrations by *Christopher Stone*
Acquisitions Editor: *Connie Kallback*
Production Editor: *Mariann Hutlak*
Interior Design/Formatting: *Dee Coroneos*

Printed in the United States of America

10   9   8   7   6   5   4   3   2   1

ISBN 0-87628-135-8

**THE CENTER FOR APPLIED RESEARCH
IN EDUCATION**
West Nyack, NY 10994
A Simon & Schuster Company

On the World Wide Web at http://www.phdirect.com

Prentice Hall International (UK) Limited, *London*
Prentice Hall of Australia Pty. Limited, *Sydney*
Prentice Hall Canada, Inc., *Toronto*
Prentice Hall Hispanoamericana, S.A., *Mexico*
Prentice Hall of India Private Limited, *New Delhi*
Prentice Hall of Japan, Inc., *Tokyo*
Simon & Schuster Asia Pte. Ltd., *Singapore*
Editora Prentice Hall do Brasil, Ltda., *Rio de Janeiro*

Dedication

This book is dedicated to our families. Our parents, Peggy Walker and J.P. and Helen Rowe, have always encouraged us and supported our efforts. To assist us, they have researched and collected information from every imaginable source. They help us stay abreast of current developments in science.

Matthew, Audrey, and Spencer McGhee are three loving and supportive individuals who have endured us through many projects. Without their constant emotional and physical help, we would have run low on the psychic energy needed to teach school and write at the same time.

Acknowledgments

This book has been influenced by many people. A summer visit to the Georgia Bureau of Investigation was arranged by Margaret Arnold, Douglas County School System's Apprenticeship Coordinator. Scientists, computer experts, fingerprint analysts, and management at the GBI took time out of their hectic schedules to show us everything we wanted to see.

By inviting us to attend our first Biennial Chemistry Conference, Maureen Schuberg provided us with opportunities to learn new science techniques and teaching methods. Through the conference, we met teachers working at all levels of science education who shared their ideas and concerns about increasing student interest in science.

Connie Kallback, our editor, was willing to give us a chance to try something new. She never got tired of answering questions and helping us meet deadlines. Her encouragement and approval kept our spirits high and our pen aimed in the right direction.

Diane Turso, our Development Editor, did an excellent job preparing the manuscript for print. Without her expertise we would not have looked so professional.

The artwork was beautifully done by Christopher Stone. Chris was able to create Crime Cat and draw him in interesting investigative poses. Without Chris's creative flair, this book would have lacked some of its appeal.

About the Authors

Pam Walker (B.S., biology, Georgia College; M.Ed. and Ed.S., Georgia Southern University) has 15 years' experience in teaching science in grades 9–12.

Elaine Wood (A.B., biology and secondary education; M.S. and Ed.S., West Georgia College) has conducted research on the cellular and molecular level and has 10 years' teaching experience in secondary science.

Ms. Walker and Ms. Wood teach science at Alexander High School in Douglasville, Georgia. They are co-authors of several teacher resource books, including *Handbooks for Applied Biology/Chemistry* to accompany the CORD modules, *Take Home Experiments* by Frank Schaeffer Publishing, and *Scientific Investigations* and *Science Up to Standards* by Instructional Fair/TS Dennison. They have also helped fashion a new curriculum for applied science classes by creating two new texts: *Biology in Our Lives* and *Chemistry in Our Lives* from Interstate Publishing. Their earlier science resource with The Center is *Hands-on General Science Activities With Real-Life Applications* (1994).

About This Book

Students learn best when they are interested in the topic being presented. One exciting way for students to see science is through the eyes of the crime scene investigator. Investigators are well-trained observers who are called to the scene of a crime to collect as much evidence as possible. This evidence can include samples of body fluids and fibers, casts of shoe and tire prints, measurements of crime scenes, collection of insects, and hundreds of other procedures. Oftentimes, these same investigators help detectives interpret the evidence they have collected. By stepping into the roles of crime scene investigators, students can learn numerous scientific strategies and skills.

Crime Scene Investigations can be used to supplement and energize your current science curriculum. No matter what branch of science you teach, there are lessons in this book to help you engage students in active learning. These activities help teachers make strong cross-curriculum links with other disciplines such as math, sociology, and writing.

The resource is divided into four sections, each one covering a different branch of science. Section 1, "Critical-Thinking Lessons," reinforces skills of observation, experimentation, and logical thinking. Section 2, "Physical Science Lessons," employs techniques such as analysis of unknown mixtures. Section 3, "Life Science Lessons," concentrates on evidence left at crime scenes by living things, and teaches principles of inheritance, DNA analysis, skeletal structure, and characteristics of hair and skin. Section 4, "Earth Science, Archaeology, and Anthropology Lessons," shows how reconstruction of past events and knowledge of the soil's composition can influence the outcome of a criminal investigation.

Within each section are several lessons, each of which are composed of two parts:

a. information that explains the history and current uses of the topic taught in that lesson, and a true or realistic scenario explaining how science is pivotal in solving the mystery

b. a lab on the same material, in which students are members of criminal investigative teams working on a solution to the mystery

Follow the cartoon character, Crime Cat, through the book as he introduces each new lesson to your students. Students will be intrigued by the "Who Done It?" scenarios that introduce the unsolved mystery in each lab. As students are challenged by these activities, they learn to take science techniques seriously, allowing them to think like successful crime scene investigators.

We hope you will enjoy teaching with this resource as much as we have enjoyed creating it.

Pam Walker
Elaine Wood

Contents

SECTION 1
CRITICAL-THINKING LESSONS

SECTION 2
PHYSICAL SCIENCE LESSONS

SECTION 3
LIFE SCIENCE LESSONS

SECTION 4
EARTH SCIENCE, ARCHAEOLOGY, AND ANTHROPOLOGY LESSONS

Lesson and Lab Titles	*Subject Tie-in with General Science*

Sociology, Math, Chemistry, Criminology

Sociology, Math, Chemistry, Criminology

CRITICAL-THINKING LESSONS

LESSON 1-1: WHO WROTE THIS?

A LESSON ON DOCUMENT FORGERY

Could you select your signature if it were mixed in with a group of similar signatures? When you get a letter in the mail, can you identify its author from the handwriting? Because handwriting is very individualistic, you can usually recognize your own handwriting and that of a good friend.

Handwriting Analysis

Handwriting analysis can be used in forensic science to establish whether or not forgery has been committed. Forgery is the illegal act of reproducing someone's signature without his or her permission. Forgery is most commonly encountered when an individual illegally signs another person's name to a check to steal money from that person's checking account. Experts in handwriting, who are also called document examiners, often testify in court about the author of a signature.

Handwriting comparison is the most frequently requested type of document analysis. As people mature, they develop personal habits that contribute to unique characteristics in their handwriting. By adulthood, a person's handwriting is as exclusive to them as their speech. Even when a person tries to disguise his or her handwriting, some of that person's own characteristics can still be seen. When experts in handwriting carefully compare two documents, they can usually tell whether the documents were written by the same person.

No Two the Same

Handwriting comparisons are useful because no two people have exactly the same handwriting. When the signature of a person on a check is questioned, the handwriting expert looks at the class and individual characteristics of the letters in that signature. The class characteristics are the features and dimensions of the letters, such as the connections of letters to each other, the capitalization, and the punctuation. The individual characteristics are the unique features of the letters. For example, is the "o" in the signature open at the top? Is the "n" written with a pointed tip? Individual characteristics are often the keys to detecting forgery, because these are very hard to duplicate. There are some key characteristics that document examiners always look for, such as broken strokes, wavering lines, retouching of parts of a letter, changes in writing speed, and overemphasis on strokes.

Compare It with the Standard

When the handwriting in a document is in question, the document examiner asks for a handwriting sample with which to compare the questioned document. This sample is the standard for comparison. A standard is usually obtained from two sources: requested writing and collected writing. The collected writing comes from writing done *before* the investigation began. It may be signatures on canceled checks or written applications for jobs. To provide a requested writing, an individual writes a dictated text using the same type of paper and ink that was used in the document in question.

Twelve Basic Characteristics for Comparing Handwriting

Experts usually examine the following characteristics when examining handwriting samples:

1. Line quality: Do the letters flow or are they written with very intent strokes?

2. Spacing of words and letters: What is the average space between words and letters?

3. Ratio of height, width, and size of letters: Are the letters consistent in height, width, and size?

4. Lifting pen: Does the author lift his or her pen to stop writing a word and start a new word?

5. Connecting strokes: How are capital letters connected to lower-case letters?

6. Strokes to begin and end: Where does the letter begin and end on a page?

7. Unusual letter formation: Are any letters written with unusual slants or angles? Are some letters printed rather than written in cursive?

8. Pen pressure: How much pen pressure is applied on upward and downward strokes?

9. Slant: Do letters slant to the left or right? If slant is pronounced, a protractor may be used to determine the degree.

10. Baseline habits: Does the author write on the line or does the writing go above or below the line?

11. Fancy writing habits: Are there any unusual curls or loops or unique styles?

12. Placement of diacritics: How does the author cross the t's or dot the i's?

Figure 1 gives examples of different writing styles showing variations in the 12 criteria for examination.

1. Line quality:

Smooth- *Jack and Jill went ~~up~~ the hill.*

Shaky or nervous- *Jack and Jill werat up the hill.*

Juvenile or deliberate-

Jack and Jill went up the hill.

2. Spacing:

Left margin is even:

Our business in Switzerland is great. We are grossing over one million dollars a year. We know this will double by the next decade.

Left margin is jagged:

Our business in Switzerland is great. We are grossing over one million dollars a year. We know this will double by the next decade.

Angle on left margin:

Our business in Switzerland is great. We are grossing over one million dollars a year. We know this will double by the next decade.

Angle on right margin:

Our business in Switzerland is great. We are grossing over one million dollars a year. We know this will double by the next decade.

Space between capital letters and small letters:

Jack and Jill went up the hill.

Space between capital letters:

Jr. P. Stevens

Space between word formations:

Jack _ and _ Jill _ went _ up _ the _ hill,

Figure 1. Variation in the 12 criteria of handwriting analysis.

3. Size and proportion:
Height of overall writing:

Jack and Jill went to the hill.

Height of short to tall letters: —

Jack and Jill went up the hill.

Evidence of diminishing strokes:

Jack and Jill went up the hill.

Evidence of increasing strokes:

Jack and Jill went up the hill.

4. Penlifts:
Removes pen entirely before starting new word:

Jack and Jill went up the hill.

Pen continues on paper close to next word:

Jackand Jill.— went up the hill.

5. Connecting strokes, ending, and beginning strokes:
Do they begin as flourished or embellished?

My

Do they end flourished?

My

Do they begin as inflexible and straight?

M

Do they end abruptly?

Cat

6. Does the letter begin at the top of the page?
Does it continue to the end of the page?

Does it stop or start in the middle?

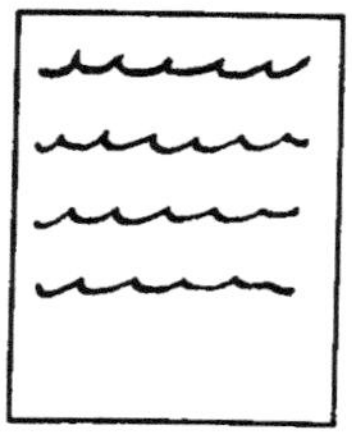

7. Any unusual letter formation?

d a p y

Figure 1. *Continued*

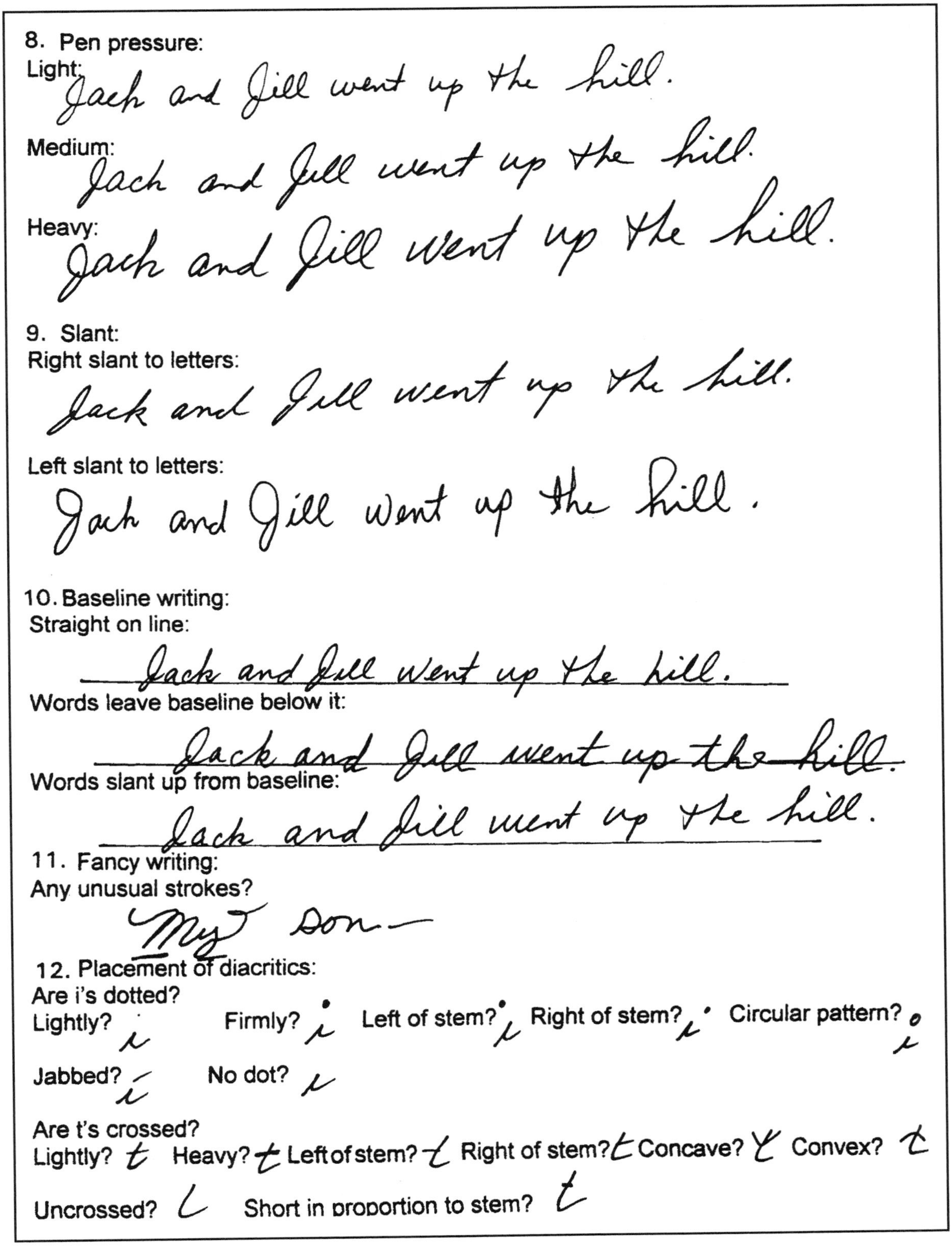

8. Pen pressure:

Light:

Jack and Jill went up the hill.

Medium:

Jack and Jill went up the hill.

Heavy:

Jack and Jill went up the hill.

9. Slant:

Right slant to letters:

Jack and Jill went up the hill.

Left slant to letters:

Jack and Jill went up the hill.

10. Baseline writing:

Straight on line:

Jack and Jill went up the hill.

Words leave baseline below it:

Jack and Jill went up the hill.

Words slant up from baseline:

Jack and Jill went up the hill.

11. Fancy writing:

Any unusual strokes?

My Son —

12. Placement of diacritics:

Are i's dotted?

Lightly? *ı*   Firmly? *ı*   Left of stem? *ı*   Right of stem? *ı*   Circular pattern? *ı*

Jabbed? *ı*   No dot? *ı*

Are t's crossed?

Lightly? *t* Heavy? *t* Left of stem? *t* Right of stem? *t* Concave? *t* Convex? *t*

Uncrossed? *t*   Short in proportion to stem? *t*

Figure 1. *Continued*

Teacher Notes and Key for Lab 1-1, *Write On!*

1. This lab requires 15 minutes on Day 1 and 45 minutes on Day 2.

2. After students endorse the check on Day 1, choose one student signature to play the role of the "forged" signature on Julian Harston's check. Make enough copies of this endorsement to give one to each lab group.

3. Before lab begins on Day 2, have students endorse another copy of this check, and place their checks at the front of the room. This gives each lab group a bank of requested writing with which they can compare the forged signature.

Answers to Postlab Questions

Student answers to the postlab questions will vary, depending on which student signature you chose to be the forged signature. Following is a suggested evaluation rubric.

EVALUATION RUBRIC

Name(s) _____ Date _____

Criteria	Points Possible	Points Earned
Analysis of document in question completed	33.3	_____
Postlab questions completed	33.3	_____
Forged check correctly identified	33.4	_____
Total	100.0	_____

Name _____ Date _____

WRITE ON!

A Lab on Document Forgery

Objective

You will analyze handwriting on a questioned document to determine the author of the document.

Background Information

Royston Textiles called the state bureau of investigation last week to report a problem with one of their canceled checks. This check was made out to their consultant, Julian Harston. It had been mailed to him more than a month ago. However, Mr. Harston reported that he never received the check. Yet, the canceled check was in Royston Textiles' bank statement this month. It had been endorsed.

Mr. Harston feels that someone in his neighborhood took the check from his mailbox and forged his name on the back. Today you are provided with copies of Julian Harston's signature written by people in his neighborhood. Your job is to decide which signature most closely matches the one on the check. This decision will help you determine if the check endorsement was forged.

Materials

Stereomicroscope or hand lens
Unlined white paper
Document in question
Black pens, all of same brand, one per lab group
Protractor (*optional*)
Ruler
Paper clip
Notebook paper
Scissors

Procedure, Day 1

1. In Figure 2 you see a check that has been written with a typewriter. It is made out to Julian Harston and signed with a Royston Textile stamp.

2. Cut out the check with scissors.

3. Turn the check over and write the name Julian Harston on the back.

4. Write your name on a piece of notebook paper and attach the check to this notebook paper with a paper clip. Give this to your teacher.

Procedure, Day 2

1. Your teacher has selected one of the checks that was turned in yesterday and made several copies of the back of that check for each lab group. In today's lab, your copy of that check is referred to as "the document in question."

2. Each person in your lab group should cut out the check in Figure 3 and sign the name Julian Harston to the back in his or her own handwriting. Write your name on a piece of notebook paper and attach the check to the notebook paper with a paper clip. Place this on the table at the front of the room, so that each person's paper is side by side.

3. Your lab group is a team of handwriting examiners. Using the information in the Background, the document in question provided by the teacher, microscope, ruler, and protractor, examine the check your teacher handed out to you today. Complete the "Analysis of the Document in Question."

4. Taking turns with other lab groups, compare the checks at the front of the room with this analysis. Determine which student committed the forgery.

Postlab Questions

1. In your opinion, who forged the check?

   _____

   _____

   _____

2. Give the main points, according to the 12 criteria, that helped you make this determination.

   _____

   _____

   _____

3. Are you so confident of your decision that you would testify in court?

   _____

   _____

   _____

4. List two checks that looked similar to the original. What helped rule out these two checks?

   _____

   _____

   _____

```
                                                              34566
                                        June 14, 1999

Royston Textiles

PAY  Julian Harston                                   $ 2,546.12

     Two thousand five hundred forty-six and 12/100      Dollars

Consultant fee                          Royston Textile Corporation
```

Figure 2. Day 1.

```
                                                              34566
                                        June 14, 1999

Royston Textiles

PAY  Julian Harston                                   $ 2,546.12

     Two thousand five hundred forty-six and 12/100      Dollars

Consultant fee                          Royston Textile Corporation
```

Figure 3. Day 2.

ANALYSIS OF THE DOCUMENT IN QUESTION

Name of Experts _____ *Date Examined* _____

_____

Criteria for examination   Notes

1. Color of ink used by person forging the check: _____

_____

2. Handwriting style: Are all parts written in cursive or are some letters printed? _____

_____

3. Description of quality of stroke: Is it smooth, nervous, or jittery? _____

_____

4. Description of spacing of margins and spacing between words: _____

_____

5. Are the letters similar in size? _____

_____

6. Describe any penlifts between words: _____

_____

7. Does the author write along a straight line or does he/she write up- or downhill? _____

_____

8. Description of unusual or fancy strokes: _____

_____

9. Describe the i's and t's in the signature: _____

_____

10. Do the letters slant? If so, in what direction? _____

_____

11. Is the pen pressure light, medium, or heavy? _____

_____

12. Any additional observations you made: _____

_____

LESSON 1-2: TYPEWRITER PERSONALITY
A LESSON ON TYPEWRITER COMPARISON

Have you ever seen a television mystery in which the criminal sent a ransom note in the form of a typed message? The bad guy used a typewriter to avoid having his or her handwriting analyzed. However, things backfired when the criminal was apprehended because the typewriter on which the ransom note was written made unusual marks, such as incomplete "p"s or crooked "m"s.

In real life, criminal investigators who work with ransom notes also analyze the impressions in the paper and the type to determine the make and model of the typewriter. Such analysis can be done by comparing the ransom note with class standards of typewriters provided by manufacturers. Unfortunately, there are so many models of typewriters and word processors today that this is an extremely difficult task for the document examiner.

One by One

The document examiner obtains samples of type and serial numbers from different typewriters and goes about the painstaking process of trying to make a match. Each typewriter has its own special quirks that make its characters unique. When the document examiner finds a match between the ransom note and a typewriter, he or she then identifies the model and make. If the document examiner can obtain the serial number from the manufacturer, he or she may be able to determine who purchased the machine. Finding that make and model of machine in a suspect's possession helps make a good case against that person.

TEACHER NOTES AND KEY FOR LAB 1-2, TATTLE-TALE TYPE

This lab requires 30 minutes.

Answers to Postlab Questions

1. Yes

2. Billy Akers

3. Answers may vary. It was easy to match the "J"s and "t"s.

4. A mechanical impression is made when a document is placed in a machine.

5. The investigators compare the ransom note with class standards provided by type-writer manufacturers.

Name _____ Date _____

Tattle-Tale Type
A Lab on Typewriter Comparison

Objective

You will use the stereomicroscope to observe and compare samples of type and determine which typewriter was used to write a ransom note.

Background Information

Little Becky Larsen was 10 years old on May 12. That day, her friends attended a birthday party at her home. When the party was over, Becky remained in the backyard to play on her new swing set. Jane Larsen, her mother, went inside the house to clean up the mess.

When Jane went to the back door to check on Becky, she was shocked to see the swing empty. After calling Becky repeatedly with no response, Jane dialed the police. Even though the police found no clues concerning Becky's whereabouts, they could not issue a Missing Person report for 24 hours. As Jane was escorting the police out the front door, a white envelope with Jane's name on it fell from the front door screen.

Jane opened the note and found the following message inside:

> Put ten thousand dollars in a brown paper bag.
>
> Place the bag in the back seat of a black Jaguar
>
> that will be parked in front of the post office on
>
> Woodston Street between 10:00 AM
>
> and 10:10 AM tomorrow morning.
>
> This is your only chance. If you fail to deliver
>
> the ransom money, you will never see your
>
> daughter again!

Jane could not believe her eyes. Who would do such a thing? After speaking at length with police, she managed to give them a list of 20 people with whom she had recently experienced problems. Because Jane is the owner of a group of apartment buildings in the city, she is forced to reprimand some tenants when they refuse to follow the rules.

The police visited and interviewed these 20 individuals and asked them to type a simple message on the typewriters they had in their homes. The police gave the document examiner a copy of these typewritten messages and a copy of the ransom note to try to establish a match.

Materials

Stereomicroscope or hand lens
Ruler

Procedure

1. Examine the typewritten messages from the 20 people Jane gave as possible suspects (Figure 4). Use the stereomicroscope or hand lens to get a closer look.

2. Examine the ransom note and compare it with the typewritten messages.

3. Determine if one of these messages is written in the same type as the ransom note.

Postlab Questions

1. Do you believe beyond a reasonable doubt that one of these individuals was in possession of a typewriter that typed the ransom note?

   _____

   _____

2. In your opinion, who is the criminal?

   _____

   _____

3. Explain why you selected this individual. What letters or characteristics led you to your conclusion?

   _____

   _____

4. What is a mechanical impression?

   _____

   _____

5. How do investigators determine the make and model of a typewriter used to write a ransom note?

   _____

   _____

Jack and Jill went up the hill to fetch a pail of water.   Mary Johnson

Jack and Jill went up the hill to fetch a pail of water.   Jack Thomas

Jack and Jill went up the hill to fetch a pail of water.   Bill Jakes

Jack and Jill went up the hill to fetch a pail of_water.   Missy Johnson

Jack and Jill went up the hill to fetch a pail of water.   Darren Olson

Jack and Jill went up the hill to fetch a pail of water.   Jimmy Jones

Jack and Jill went up the hill to fetch a pail of water.   Andy Jackson

Jack and Jill went up the hill to fetch a pail of water.   Lori Jay

Jack and Jill went up the hill to fetch a pail of water.   Keith Wilson

Jack and Jill went up the hill to fetch a pail of water.   Peggy Walker

Jack and Jill went up the hill to fetch a pail of water.   Bill Gilder

Jack and Jill went up the hill to fetch a pail of water.   Jo Anne

Jack and Jill went up the hill to fetch a pail of water.   Betty McDuffie

Jack and Jill went up the hill to fetch a pail of water.   Helen Cook

Jack and Jill went up the hill to fetch a pail of water.   Spencer Rowe

Jack and Jill went up the hill to fetch a pail of water.   Audrey McGhee

Jack and Jill went up the hill to fetch a pail of water.   Jayne Foss

Jack and Jill went up the hill to fetch a pail of water.   Lori Thomas

Jack and Jill went up the hill to fetch a pail of water.   Billy Akers

Jack and Jill went up the hill to fetch a pail of water.   Sim Edwards

Figure 4. The names of the suspects and their typewritten messages.

LESSON 1-3: BLEEDING MIXTURES
A LESSON ON CHROMATOGRAPHY OF MIXTURES

At crime scenes, investigators often find unknown materials that need to be identified. If an unknown material is a mixture, an investigator may want to know one of two things about it: What are the ingredients of the mixture? Is the mixture found at the scene the same as a known mixture?

A mixture is a collection of two or more pure substances that are physically close together. You are familiar with a variety of mixtures. For example, a soft drink is a mixture of water, sugar, artificial colors, caffeine, and flavors. Other mixtures include foods, drugs, cosmetics, fuels, lubricants, and dyes.

Black Ink Is Colorful

You may not realize it, but black ink is a mixture of several different colors. If you doubt this, write your name on a paper napkin with a black felt-tip pen. Dip the end of the napkin in water and watch the black ink separate into colors when the water reaches it. This is a simple example of ink chromatography. The colored pattern that forms on the napkin is called a chromatograph.

Chromatography is an ancient method of separating parts of a mixture. The word chromatography really means "color writing." The inks in modern pens are made of a mixture of dyes. These inks show a variety of colors when a solvent, such as water, passes through them.

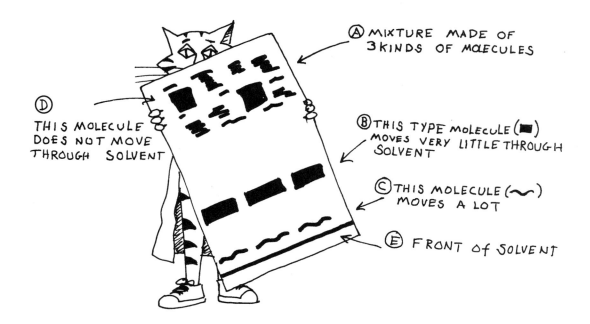

Color in Chromatograms

Different types of water-soluble ink pens vary in their composition. Two different brands of pens will give two disimilar chromatograms. Therefore, if ink samples are taken from separate locations on a document that was written with one pen, all samples should produce the same chromatogram. By using chromatography, forensic scientists can determine whether a document contains two or more different inks. One drawback of using ink chromatography in forensic science is that it destroys the evidence. The document under suspicion must have areas cut from it so the ink can be analyzed.

All the Same

In summary, if an entire document has been written with the same ink pen, then tests applied to different portions of the document should produce the same results. If the chromatograms produced are the same, the forensic scientist can assume the inks are the same.

Diverse solvents can be used in ink chromatography. For inks that are water soluble, water is the solvent of choice. For inks that are not soluble in water, methanol, ammonium hydroxide, ethanol, acetone, or hydrochloric acid can be used as solvents.

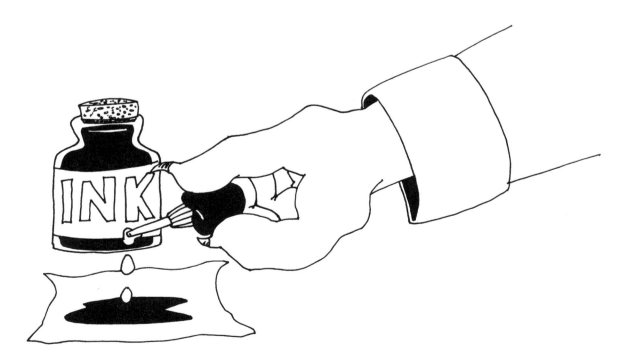

TEACHER NOTES AND KEY FOR LAB 1-3A, *DID PETE CHEAT?*

1. This lab requires 50 minutes.

2. Use two water-soluble, black felt-tip pens for this activity. Each pen should be a different brand.

3. Prepare three pieces of chromatogram (filter) paper for each lab group. To do this, cut out three long strips of filter paper. Cut one end of the paper so it forms a point. Place an ink mark about two inches above the pointed end. Also do this for the other two paper strips. You can use the same ink pen on all three strips if you want Pete to be innocent. If you want him to be guilty of changing his receipts, use one pen to make two chromatograms, and another pen to make the third one for each lab group. Each lab group will get three of these strips. Indicate to students that you cut these strips from suspicious locations on Pete's receipts.

Answers to Postlab Questions

1. If Pete is innocent, all three chromatograms will look alike. If he changed some numbers with a different pen, one of the chromatograms will be different.

2. Answers will vary, depending on whether or not you used different pens.

3. If the ink is not water soluble, you must use another solvent such as methanol.

4. The teacher could perform chromatography on it to see if the suspicious answer was written in the same ink as the original answers.

TEACHER NOTES AND KEY FOR LAB 1-3B, *WHOSE LIPSTICK?*

1. Students will need about 50 minutes to complete this lab.

2. Acetone can be bought in hardware and department stores. Before the day of the lab, test several different kinds of lipstick to see if they contain components that are soluble in alcohol. (Lipsticks that are acetone soluble include Elizabeth Arden, Anna Bella, Coty, Estee Lauder, Max Factor, Cover Girl, Avon, Maybelline, and Revlon.) Choose three acetone-soluble lipsticks and label them B, C, and D. **CAUTION:** Acetone is flammable.

3. Cut coffee filters or chromatography paper into long, thin strips. Each lab group will need four strips: one with a sample of lipstick A, the crime-scene lipstick, and three clean strips. To prepare crime-scene chromatography strips, place a dot of lipstick A on a strip of filter or chromatography paper. Be sure that the crime-scene lipstick (A) is the same as either lipstick B, C, or D.

4. Information in the Data Table should show students which lipstick sample matches sample A.

Answers to Postlab Questions

1. In this lab, the acetone is the solvent that dissolves the lipsticks.

2. Water could not have been used. Lipsticks are designed to be insoluble in water so that they will stay on the lips.

3. The answer depends on which lipstick you used as the crime sample.

4. Answers may vary. The determination that someone was present in a location before a crime was committed does not necessarily tie that person to the crime.

5. Answers will vary, but could include inks, cosmetics, dyes, food colorings, and lubricants.

Name _____ Date _____

Did Pete Cheat?
A Lab on Chromatography of Inks

Objective

You will use chromatography to determine whether a document in question was written with one or two ink pens.

Background Information

Pete Greer owns a computer business and he has become quite successful in the last several years. To save money, Pete refuses to hire an accountant to help him file his income taxes. When preparing his taxes, however, Pete can rarely find the receipts that verify the deductions he claimed as business expenses.

About a month ago, Pete received a card from the IRS notifying him that his income taxes for the last four years were going to be audited. Pete was instructed to gather all his supporting documentation and bring it with him to the IRS auditor's office.

Pete panicked and began collecting everything he could find. He found some of the receipts from the purchase of computer equipment for the new business. However, he could not find them all. Pete was not sure that he had all of the documents he needed to back up the numbers he filed on his taxes. He considered changing the amounts on several of the receipts. He thought, "I'll use this black felt-tip pen and change some of those 3's to 8's. No one will ever know the difference. In fact, they may end up owing *me* some money!"

Did Pete change any of the numbers on the receipts that verify his business expenses? You are the forensic scientist who must answer this question.

Materials

Large beaker
Straight piece of coat hanger or stiff wire
Hole puncher
Water
3 paper clips
Ruler
Pencil
3 pieces of filter paper with ink samples from the questioned document
Paper towels

Procedure

1. Obtain three pieces of filter paper with ink samples on them. These three papers were taken from three separate locations on one of Pete's suspicious receipts.

© 1998 by The Center for Applied Research in Education

2. Use a hole puncher to make a hole in each piece of paper at the end *opposite* the ink mark.

3. Thread a piece of stiff wire through the holes in the three pieces of paper. Make sure the pieces of paper do not touch each other when they hang from the wire.

4. Place a paper clip at the pointed end of each piece of paper. This will keep the pieces of paper from curling.

5. Lower the three pieces of paper into a beaker. Rest the stiff wire across the top of the beaker so the three samples are hanging into the beaker but not touching the bottom of the beaker.

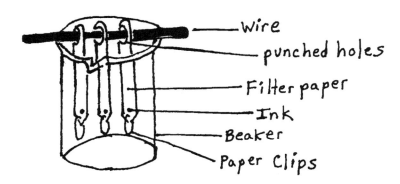

6. Carefully add water to the beaker until it covers the paper clips and makes contact with the pointed ends of the papers. Do not add so much water that it covers the ink marks on the papers.

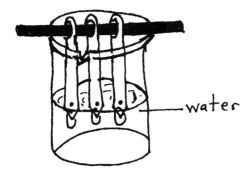

7. Leave this beaker undisturbed until the solvent has dampened most of each piece of paper.

8. Remove the wire and the three pieces of paper. Place the three pieces of paper on a paper towel to dry.

9. Once dry, staple the three pieces of paper (which are chromatograms) to your Postlab Questions.

Postlab Questions for Lab 1-3A

1. Staple the three chromatograms to this page.

Postlab Questions for Lab 1-3A (continued)

2. Did Pete change his receipts to keep from paying more money to the IRS? Support your answer.

   _____

   _____

   _____

   _____

   _____

   _____

   _____

   _____

3. Is water always a good solvent in ink separation? Explain your answer.

   _____

   _____

   _____

   _____

   _____

   _____

   _____

4. How could a teacher use ink chromatography to determine whether or not a student has changed his or her answers after a test has been graded and returned?

   _____

   _____

   _____

   _____

   _____

   _____

   _____

Name _____ Date _____

Whose Lipstick?
A Lab on Chromatography of Lipstick

Objective

You will use the technique of paper chromatography to compare lipstick from a suspect with known lipstick samples.

Background Information

Mr. Sternman was a very unpopular man who had managed to make enemies of everyone he knew. Even his own family found him to be an unbearable bully who lied, cheated, and stole from his wife and grown daughter. Mr. Sternman had scheduled a meeting with his new attorney, Ms. Justice, on the afternoon that he was found dead in his apartment.

After being exiled from his home a year ago, Mr. Sternman had moved into a beautiful apartment downtown. Because he was so mean, no one ever visited him. He hated house cleaning and his apartment became a shamble. On the day that his body was found, one scene in the apartment was notable because it was so unusual. The dining room table was laid out with a fresh tablecloth and silver candelabra. Two cups of coffee, two napkins, and a plate of cookies were on the table. One of the napkins contained a smear of lipstick.

In this lab, you will analyze the lipstick on the napkin and compare it with the lipstick of the only three women who were known to have visited Mr. Sternman's apartment: his wife, Mrs. Sternman; his daughter, Miss Sternman; and his attorney, Ms. Justice.

Materials

Paper strip containing lipstick sample from crime scene (A)
Paper strip containing lipstick sample from daughter (B)
Paper strip containing lipstick sample from wife (C)
Paper strip containing lipstick sample from attorney (D)
Acetone (about 10 ml) **CAUTION:** Be careful! Acetone is flammable.
3 strips of filter or chromatography paper
Scissors
Beakers or plastic cups
Tape
Goggles

Procedure

1. Your teacher has cut the lipstick-smeared crime-scene napkin into several strips. Obtain one of these strips and label the end *opposite* the lipstick sample as A.

2. Obtain three strips of filter paper. On one end, label one strip as "B," one as "C," and one as "D."

3. On the other end of each strip of paper, about 2 centimeters from the end of the strip, place a small dot of the appropriate lipstick.

4. Carefully pour 10 ml of acetone into the beaker or cup.

5. Place all four strips of paper in the acetone so that the lipstick end of each strip is just touching the acetone. (Do not let any acetone get on the lipstick.) Fold the opposite end of each strip of paper over the top of the cup or beaker. Secure with tape, if necessary.

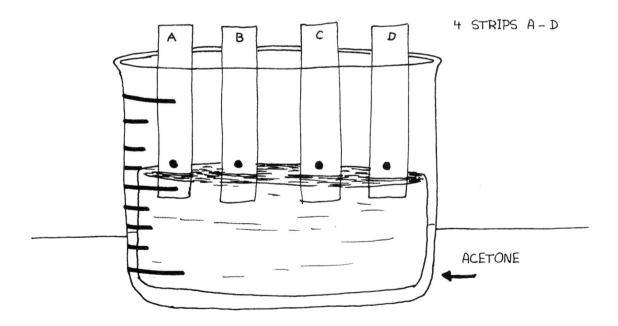

6. After 15 minutes, remove all the samples from the beaker. Measure the distance the acetone moved up each strip of paper. Also measure the distance each component of the lipsticks moved up the paper. Some lipsticks have only two or three components, and some have more. Enter these measurements on the Data Table.

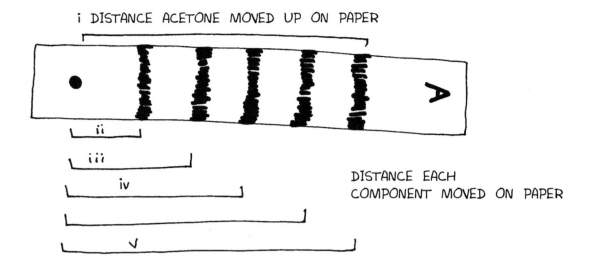

i DISTANCE ACETONE MOVED UP ON PAPER

DISTANCE EACH
COMPONENT MOVED ON PAPER

7. Determine the R_f for each lipstick component of all lipstick samples. Enter those values on the Data Table. The R_f is calculated by dividing the distance traveled by each lipstick component by the distance traveled by the acetone.

$$R_f = \frac{\text{Distance traveled by one lipstick component}}{\text{Distance traveled by solvent (acetone)}}$$

Postlab Questions for Lab 1-3B

1. In this experiment, what is the purpose of the acetone?

_____

_____

2. Do you think water could have been used in place of the acetone? Why or why not?

_____

_____

3. According to your results, who drank coffee with Mr. Sternman before he was killed?

_____

_____

4. Do you think the discovery of this person's lipstick in Mr. Sternman's apartment is enough evidence to link that person with the crime? Why or why not?

_____

_____

5. What are some other mixtures that you think can be separated by chromatography?

_____

_____

DATA TABLE

Distances (in centimeters) that acetone and lipstick components moved up the paper.

Lipstick samples	Distance acetone moved	Distance lipstick components moved	R_f
A	i.	ii.	
		iii.	
		iv.	
		v.	
B	i.	ii.	
		iii.	
		iv.	
		v.	
C	i.	ii.	
		iii.	
		iv.	
		v.	
D	i.	ii.	
		iii.	
		iv.	
		v.	

LESSON 1-4: TRACKING ON!
A LESSON ON TIRE TRACK EVALUATION

Motor vehicles are essential to all aspects of society, including the criminal aspects. Most crimes involve a motor vehicle. Often, the only evidence left at a crime scene is a tire track. Therefore, investigators carefully search crime scenes for clues left by vehicles. A tire track is the path left in the soil by the wheels of a vehicle. Sometimes, tire treads can be seen in the tracks. A tire tread is the pattern of the tread design on the tire.

To record tire tread and track evidence, the crime scene is marked with crime scene tape and protected from damage. Then the tracks are photographed, measured, and cast. Each photograph includes some item that gives the picture scale: a ruler, coin, or pen can be used. The best photographs are made straight-on to the track, as if the photographer were suspended in the air above it.

Measuring Track Width

Tire tracks can tell an investigator the direction of travel and any changes in that direction. When careful measurements are made, they can also reveal vehicle tire track width and front and rear tread patterns. The tire track width is the distance in inches between the middle of the two front tires on the two back tires of a vehicle. Track width measurements can be used to identify a type of vehicle. Tread marks are often helpful in identifying a particular vehicle within this type.

Check Out the Tread Width

Tread width is the distance in inches across the tread pattern. Vehicles often use different kinds of tires, and therefore different tread patterns, on the front and rear wheels. That is why, front and back tread widths must be measured separately.

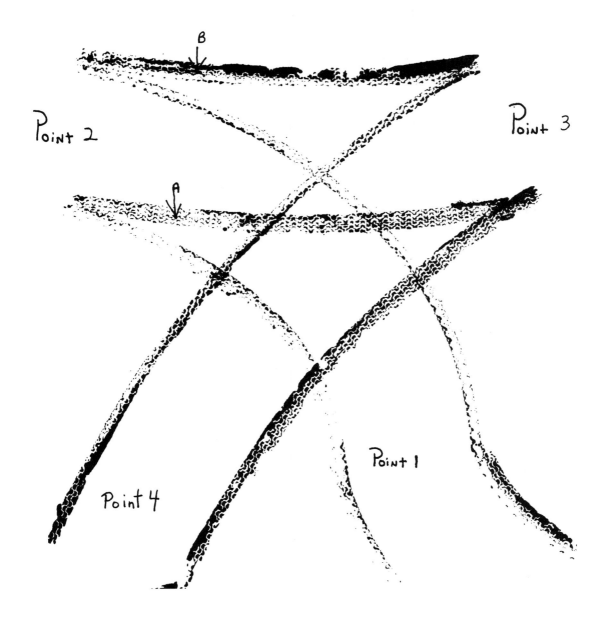

Figure 5. Distance from A to B is the wheelbase. This vehicle began at point 1, stopped at point 2, backed up to point 3, then pulled forward to point 4.

TEACHER NOTES AND KEY FOR LAB 1-4, *TREAD LIGHTLY*

1. Students need 60 minutes to complete this lab.

2. Purchase 10 toy vehicles that are similar in size. Examine the tires on these toys to be sure that the tire treads on all the cars are *similar*, but *not exactly alike*.

3. Before the lab, use one of the cars to make tire prints for every lab group. Label these prints: "Tire tracks from Sheriff Hosey's yard." Be sure the tire prints include a turn so that students can tell the difference between the front and back tires. Do not tell students which car you used to make the prints.

Answers to Postlab Questions

1. Answers will vary, depending on which car you chose to be the one that runs over Sheriff Hosey's mailbox.

2. Answers will vary, depending on the toy cars you selected.

3. Answers will vary.

4. The car that made these prints was originally moving from top to bottom. It stopped at point A, backed up to point B, moved to point C, then backed to D.

5. Any car of that make and model could have made those tracks.

Name _____ Date _____

TREAD LIGHTLY
A Lab on Tire Track Evaluation

Objectives

You will determine the track width of a vehicle by examining its tire tracks.
You will identify tires by their tread marks.

Background Information

Someone has run over Sheriff Hosey's mailbox for the third time. Even though he is a patient man, the sheriff decides to find out who keeps destroying his mailbox. This third incident occurred about 2:00 A.M. Saturday. As soon as he heard the familiar crash, the sheriff ran to his front porch to get a glimpse of the offending car and its license plate. Unfortunately, the car was moving too fast for him to read the license plate number.

The sheriff saw enough of the car, however, to narrow down his list of suspects. He knows that it was a dark-colored sports car. On the rear bumper was the familiar sticker:

> **GHS**
> **Gladville High School**

In his yard, on both sides of his crushed mailbox, are a distinctive set of tire prints.

On Monday morning, Sheriff Hosey stood in the Gladville High School parking lot and made a list of dark-colored sports cars with GHS stickers. When he had his list complete, he asked Principal Wilkins to send the students who drove these cars to the parking lot to help him make prints of their tires. He carried these prints back to his yard for comparison.

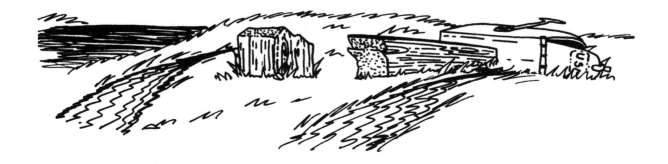

Materials

10 model cars
A print from the car that ran over Sheriff Hosey's mailbox
Ruler
Paper
Ink pad

Procedure

1. Examine the print from the car that ran over Sheriff Hosey's mailbox. Measure the tire track width (in inches) of this print and the width of the front and rear tire treads (in inches). Be very exact in your measurements. Enter all measurements on the Data Table.

2. Using white paper and the ink pad, make tire prints of suspect cars 1 through 10.

3. Measure the tire track width and tread widths of each of these cars, and enter this information on the Data Table.

Postlab Questions

1. Which car ran over Sheriff Hosey's mailbox?

   _____

   _____

2. In this lab, how many cars have tires with different tread widths on their front and rear tires?

   _____

   _____

3. Tread patterns are often very distinctive. Could you have identified the car belonging to the mailbox vandal by tread patterns?

   _____

   _____

4. Based on the tire tracks shown in the illustration, in which direction was this vehicle moving? How do you know?

   _____

   _____

5. Even though Sheriff Hosey found a car that could have made the tracks in his yard, he could not prosecute. Why not?

   _____

   _____

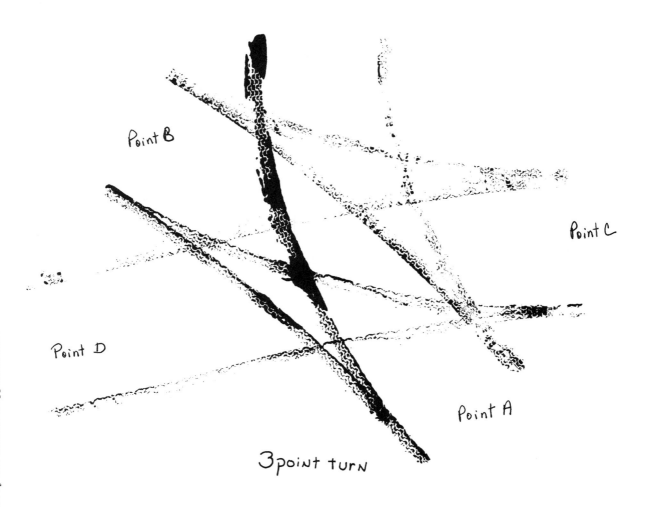

Point B

Point C

Point D

Point A

3 point turn

DATA TABLE

Wheelbase and tread width measurements.

Vehicle	Tire track width	Front tire tread width	Rear tire tread width
Print of car that ran over mailbox			
Print of car 1			
Print of car 2			
Print of car 3			
Print of car 4			
Print of car 5			
Print of car 6			
Print of car 7			
Print of car 8			
Print of car 9			
Print of car 10			

LESSON 1-5: ON THE SCENE

A LESSON ON CRIME SCENE EVALUATION

The art of forensic science begins at the crime scene. It is very important to protect and secure the area where the crime took place to ensure that evidence is not destroyed. Investigators carefully comb the crime scene for clues and evidence that later may be used in a court. In order to record the crime scene, notes are taken, photographs are made, and sketches are done. Photographs are usually the best record of the scene. However, there are times when good photographs are not possible because of environmental restrictions. In such cases, sketches and notes must be very detailed.

When possible, the crime site and adjacent locations are photographed before any other investigative work is done. All victims are photographed as they were found. The size of a body and other items are determined by placing a ruler in the photograph. Some larger police departments are replacing photography with videotaping of the crime site.

Scene Sketch

Once the photographer has completed his or her job, the crime scene investigator makes a sketch of the crime scene. The initial sketch he or she makes is a "rough" sketch that accurately represents the dimensions of the scene and shows the location of all objects that may be important in the case. These objects, which help establish that a crime was committed, are called physical evidence. To give his or her sketch scale, the investigator selects two fixed points at the crime scene. In a room, these may be the corners or windows. The investigator uses a tape measure to determine the distance of each important object in the room from both of these fixed points. These distances are recorded in the sketch (Figure 6).

Once the locations of the objects have been recorded, each object is assigned a "letter." At the bottom of the sketch, these lettered objects are identified. The sketch is also oriented to North (Figure 7). Later, a finished sketch is drawn from this rough sketch by a skilled artist. This finished sketch reflects information in the rough sketch, but is much neater (Figure 8). It may be used as evidence in the courtroom during a trial.

Note It

Notes are also taken at the scene of a crime that describe all physical evidence in detail. Notes include information about who discovered the evidence, the time that it was discovered, and how the evidence was collected and packaged. Notes must be very detailed in case they are needed to refresh someone's memory years after a crime has been committed.

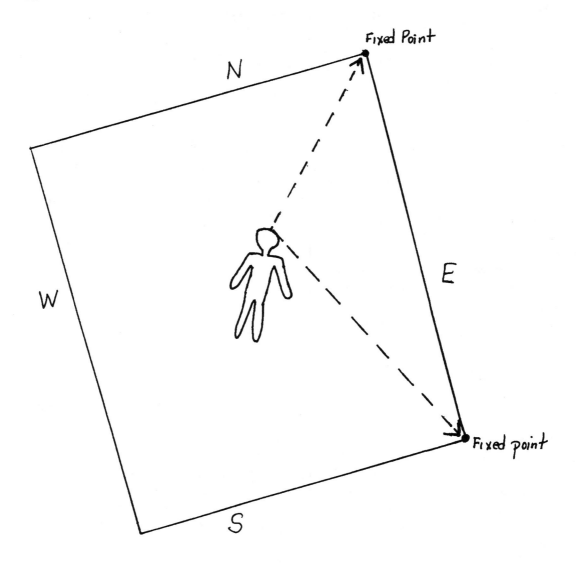

Figure 6. An investigator measures the distance between a piece of evidence and each fixed point.

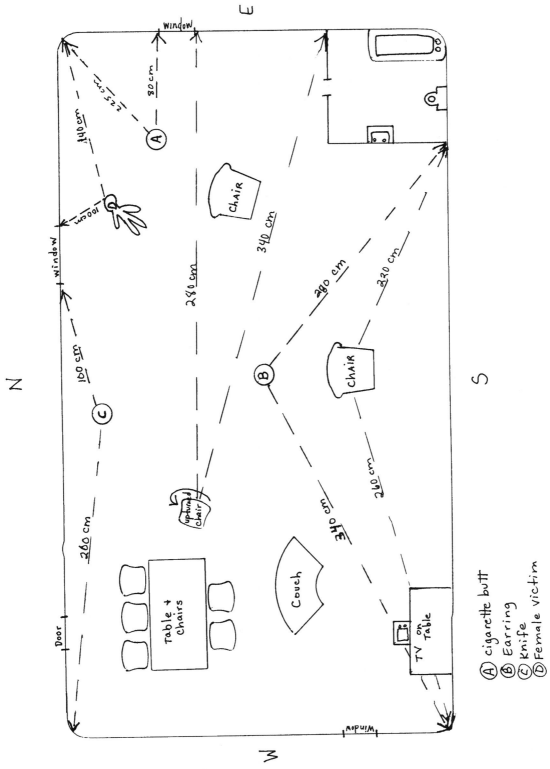

Figure 7. A sketch is oriented to north.

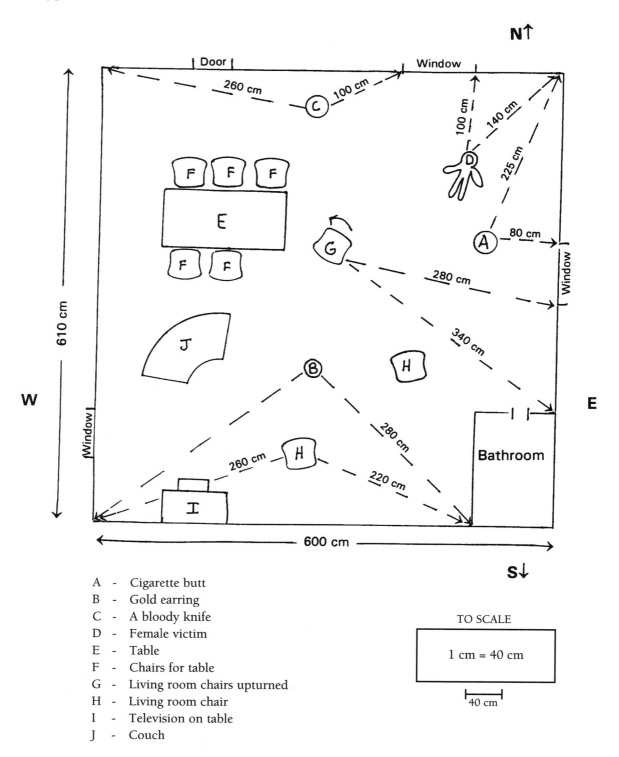

A - Cigarette butt
B - Gold earring
C - A bloody knife
D - Female victim
E - Table
F - Chairs for table
G - Living room chairs upturned
H - Living room chair
I - Television on table
J - Couch

TO SCALE

1 cm = 40 cm

40 cm

Figure 8. The finished sketch is a polished drawing of the rough sketch.

TEACHER NOTES AND KEY FOR LAB 1-5, *DON'T TOUCH THE EVIDENCE*

1. This activity will require three 50-minute class periods. The first period will be for viewing the crime scene and making the rough sketch, the second period for preparing the final draft of the sketch, and the third period for presentation of the final sketch to the class. If you prefer to shorten the activity to two 50-minute periods, have students prepare their final drafts as homework.

2. The day before the activity, set up the crime scene. This will be easier if you select a room away from your classroom. There are various ways you can set up the room, depending on the materials you have available at school. Some suggestions for a convincing crime scene include:

   ◆ Use masking tape to make an outline of the body of an adult female somewhere on the floor.

   ◆ Near the outline place a telephone whose outlet cord has been removed from the wall. Take the phone off the hook.

   ◆ Place one large earring near the outline of the body.

   ◆ Place a table in the center of the room with some chairs. Turn one chair upside down.

   ◆ Near the entrance to the room or near a window, place a cigarette butt and a tube of lipstick.

   ◆ Near the victim place a note that has been torn in pieces. When reassembled, the note might read: "Meet me at 9:00 tonight at Buck's place. Love, Sam."

   ◆ If you want to be dramatic you could scatter some ketchup (blood) near the body and perhaps near the window or door. You might even want to make a footprint (such as a woman's shoe) in ketchup in the room.

3. The day of the activity, write "Crime Scene: Do Not Enter" on a piece of wide, yellow ribbon and place it across the door of the crime scene. Before taking students to the scene, divide them into pairs called "investigative teams" and have them read the lab directions. Tell students that a murder was committed last night and that they will be investigating the scene. Explain that after today, the crime scene will be returned to normal, so they must be very detailed in their observations.

4. The second day will be spent developing the final draft of the sketch. On day 3, each team will "testify" during the "trial." Set up your classroom like a courtroom. Have an easel in the room to hold the final sketches as presenters explain what they saw to their classmates. Students may ask questions of the presenters.

5. After all presentations are complete, discuss what might have happened in the room. One interpretation could be that the deceased was romantically involved with her murderer's husband. The murderer found the note that her husband had written the deceased and went to the house of the deceased to confront her. When the deceased tried to phone for help, the wife ripped the telephone from the wall, tore the note into pieces, and threw them at her. During this time, the murderer

stabbed the victim, then fled from the scene leaving her earring, shoe print, and cigarette butt in the room.

6. The following suggested grading rubric will help you evaluate each student's work.

EVALUATION RUBRIC

Name(s) _____   Date _____

Criteria	Points Possible	Points Earned
Rough sketch completed	25	_____
Final sketch:		
Neat	5	_____
Drawn to scale	5	_____
Evidence labeled	5	_____
North labeled	5	_____
Objects in drawing proportional	5	_____
Based on rough sketch	5	_____
Presentation of sketch	20	_____
Postlab questions	25	_____
Total	100.0	_____

Answers to Postlab Questions

1. Answers will vary, depending on how you establish the crime scene.

2. Answers will vary, depending on how you establish the crime scene.

3. Fixed points cannot be mistaken by other people who are looking at the depiction of the evidence.

4. The polished drawing should be drawn more to scale and be more accurate than the rough sketch which is frequently done rapidly soon after the crime.

Name _____ Date _____

Don't Touch the Evidence
A Lab on Crime Scene Evaluation

Objective

You will draw rough and final sketches of a crime scene, and explain the scene to your classmates.

Background Information

Last night a murder was committed. The victim was identified as a 25-year-old, single, female. At 9:00 P.M., she was discovered by her neighbor. The victim had been stabbed in the chest and was lying face down when she was found. Before she was removed from the scene of the crime, the position of her body was outlined with tape. None of the other items at the scene were disturbed.

Materials

Pencil
Black pen or marker
White paper
Clipboard
Tape measure
Compass
Ruler
Prepared crime scene

Procedure, Day 1: Rough Drawing of Crime Scene

1. Accompany your partner to the room where the crime was committed.

2. Identify all items in the room that you believe to be physical evidence. Also note the taped outline of the victim on the floor.

3. Calculate locations of physical evidence for your drawing by the following method:

   a. Use the metric tape measure to determine the width and length of the room. Record these measurements in Data Table 1.

   b. Use a compass to determine which walls are north, south, east, and west.

   c. Select two fixed points in the room that are relatively close to one of the pieces of physical evidence. All victims of the crime and objects that seem out of place should be recorded as physical evidence.

d. Measure the distance (in centimeters) from one of the objects to the first fixed point. Record the name of the object and its location and distance from the fixed points in Data Table 2.

4. Repeat this procedure for all other pieces of physical evidence in the room. You do not have to use the same fixed point each time. You can change points when you change from one object to the next.

5. Using the entries you made in the data table as a guide, sketch the crime scene. As you work, follow these directions:

   a. Draw the room in which the crime occurred. Allow your sketch of the room to take up at least one-half of the paper.

   b. Indicate North on your sketch of the room.

   c. Draw all doors and windows in their proper locations.

   d. Use squares or circles to represent the locations of different objects in the room. Draw larger objects with larger squares or circles. For example, a table should be larger than a chair.

   e. Label each piece of physical evidence with a letter. At the bottom of the page, list each letter and describe the item it identifies.

   f. Beginning with Object A, draw a dashed line from one of the fixed points you chose earlier to Object A. Draw a dashed line from the other fixed point to Object A.

   g. Write the actual distances above the dashed lines on the drawing. These are the same distances you recorded in Data Table 2.

   h. Repeat steps *f* and *g* for all pieces of physical evidence in the room.

Procedure, Days 2 and 3: Final Drawing and Presentation

1. Use the "rough" sketch you made of the crime scene to draw a polished, final sketch. The final sketch will be used as evidence in a "trial."

2. The final sketch should:

   a. Be neatly drawn with black ink or marker on a piece of posterboard.

   b. Be drawn to scale. In your drawing, let 1 centimeter equal 40 centimeters of space in the room. In other words, if you measured the crime scene room to be 600 cm wide and 610 cm long, you would draw this room about 15 cm wide and a little more than 15 cm long.

   c. Label North on the drawing.

   d. Draw the squares and circles that represent physical evidence in proportion to each other. For instance, the female body should be drawn larger than the circle or square representing a knife; the tables should be larger than the body and the chairs, etc.

   e. Have the lines from the two fixed points in proportion to the rest of the drawing. Remember your scale: 1 cm equals 40 cm of actual length.

DATA TABLE 1

Measurements of room where crime occurred.

Length of room	Width of room

DATA TABLE 2

Measurement of physical evidence from fixed points.

Name of object	Fixed point 1	Fixed point 2	Distance of object from fixed point 1	Distance of object from fixed point 2
Ex.: Broken eyeglasses	Doorknob on front door	Corner where front wall meets wall on East side of house	230 cm	300 cm

f. Place the actual length and width of the room on the drawing. Use the same numbers you used in Data Table 1. Place the actual distances of the evidence from the fixed points on the dashed lines using the numbers you placed in Data Table 2.

g. Your drawing should contain all information in the rough sketch.

3. With your investigative team, present your final sketch to the class.

Postlab Questions

1. Describe any weapons found at the scene of the crime and their locations in the room.

_____

_____

_____

_____

_____

2. Describe any furniture that was upturned or items that appeared out of their normal locations.

_____

_____

_____

_____

_____

3. Why were you asked to use fixed points in your drawing?

_____

_____

_____

_____

_____

4. Why do you think you did not make your polished sketch at the crime scene?

_____

_____

_____

_____

_____

LESSON 1-6: IF THE SHOE FITS

A LESSON ON MAKING AND EVALUATING SHOE PRINT IMPRESSIONS

When shoe- or footprints are found at a crime scene, all attempts are made to preserve the impressions or their reproductions for later examination in the laboratory. Before crime scene technicians touch them, extensive photographs are made from several angles. The photographer attempts to capture specific details of the prints.

Impressions Are Not Prints

Shoe- and footprints may be found as either true prints or impressions. A print is two-dimensional while an impression is three-dimensional. Prints are made by placing material on or removing it from a hard surface, while impressions are made in pliable material. Prints are often lifted from a surface; impressions are captured for examination by casting.

Print Saver

Preservation of a true print is simple if it is made on a portable surface, such as a floor tile or piece of glass. But when the print is on a substance that cannot be carried to the lab, special lifting techniques are necessary. Footprints made in dust or dirt can be preserved by a technique similar to that used to lift a fingerprint. A lifting material is placed over the print and a roller is used to eliminate air pockets. Electrostatic charge devices are sometimes employed to lift difficult prints in the sand.

47

TEACHER NOTES AND KEY FOR LAB 1-6, CASTING FOR EVIDENCE

1. Students need 30 minutes on Day 1 and 30 minutes on Day 2.

2. Four suspect shoe prints have been provided, if you would like to use these in your lab. These prints were made from four Nike™ women's cross-training shoes, size 8. If you use these prints, you must have one of these shoes to make impressions in soft soil or clay. Ask the gym teacher to help you find one of these shoes.

3. Alternately, you can make you own shoe prints. Find four shoes that are *similar*, but *not the same*. Brush the bottom of each shoe with washable paint or food coloring, then stamp the print on a clean piece of paper. Choose one of the shoes to be the perpetrator's shoe and use it to make impressions in soil or clay. You may want to work outdoors if you make the impressions in soft soil. Modeling clay or play dough can be used to make prints indoors. The use of casting frames is not essential with modeling clay or play dough.

4. Each lab group needs a casting frame, or four pieces of plank that are 12 to 18 inches long. If planking is not available, prints made in very damp soil may become distorted by the weight of the plaster of paris. If the soil is firm, or if you use clay, the casting frame is not necessary.

Answers to Postlab Questions

1. Answers will vary, depending on which shoe you used to make the perpetrator's print.

2. The casting frame keeps the plaster of paris from distorting the shape of the print.

3. By painting the bottom of the cast with washable paint or ink, you could stamp a shoe print on a piece of white paper. This would be helpful in comparing the perpetrator's print with the four suspects' prints.

4. Answers will vary, but could include car tires, bike tires, boots, bare feet, and others.

Name _____ Date _____

CASTING FOR EVIDENCE
A Lab on Making and Evaluating Shoe Print Impressions

Objectives

You will make a cast of a shoe impression.

You will use this cast to determine whether the suspect's shoe matches prints taken from the crime scene.

Background Information

Brandon's Burger Bonanza was robbed late Saturday night several hours after closing. When the police arrived, they parked a few yards away from the restaurant. Then they surrounded the area with yellow crime scene tape to preserve the evidence.

Since on-lookers had been kept at bay, some valuable print evidence was found near the restaurant. A light rain had fallen about closing time. In the soft dirt, the robber's shoes had cast neat impressions by the back door. Investigators need a copy of those impressions to determine what size shoe the assailant wore, and what unusual markings might be found on his or her shoes.

Materials

4 suspect footprints
Ruler
An impression of the thief's footprint in clay or soft soil
Stereomicroscope
Plaster of paris
Casting frame (*optional*)
Water

Procedure, Day 1

1. If you are using a casting frame, place it around the footprint:

    a. Arrange the four pieces of plank around the footprint, getting as close to the print as possible without distorting it.

    b. Press the pieces of plank into the soil to a depth that is as deep as the print.

    c. Have the ends of the planks adjoin so that they form corners.

2. Place enough water (estimate) in a mixing bowl to fill the cast. Add powdered plaster of paris, stirring constantly, until the water and plaster reach the consistency of pancake batter. If the mixture is too thick, add more water. If it is too thin, add more plaster.

3. Holding the bowl over the impression to be cast, pour the liquid plaster of paris gently, breaking its fall into the impression with the spoon.

4. Allow the cast to sit about 30 minutes, then remove it. You should have a perfect, opposite impression of the shoe print.

5. Before the cast completely dries, mark your name and the date on it with a stylus.

6. Let the cast dry overnight.

Procedure, Day 2

1. Gently rinse any adhering soil from the cast.

2. Compare the cast you made with the four suspect footprints. To positively match your cast to a print, you must find twelve points of comparison that are the same. For example, if you find that your cast and one of the prints have the same tread pattern, that is one point of comparison that is the same. If you find that your cast and one of the prints show a tear on the heel, that is a second point of comparison that is the same.

3. As you compare your cast with the suspect's prints, list all points of comparison that are the same for the cast and each of the four prints. Record these points in the Data Table. Some points have been listed in the first column. As you study the prints and cast, add more points to this column.

DATA TABLE

Points of comparison between cast and prints that are the same.

Points of comparison	Print 1	Print 2	Print 3	Print 4
Tread pattern				
Length				
Width				

Postlab Questions

1. Which print matched your cast? How many points of comparison matched between your cast and this print?

_____

_____

_____

_____

_____

_____

2. What was the purpose of the casting frame?

_____

_____

_____

_____

_____

_____

3. How could you use your cast to make a shoe print? Would this be helpful in the investigation? Why or why not?

_____

_____

_____

_____

_____

_____

4. What other kinds of impressions might be helpful in solving a crime?

_____

_____

_____

_____

_____

_____

Suspect Shoe Print # 1.

Suspect Shoe Print #2.

Suspect Shoe Print #3.

Suspect Shoe Print #4.

LESSON 1-7: I'M CLUELESS
A LESSON ON DEDUCTIVE REASONING

Have you ever played the board game **Clue**™? In this game, players gather information in order to determine the murderer, murder weapon, and crime scene. Actually, participants are not "guessing" when they play this game; they are using deductive reasoning. As players gather more information, they begin to put together the pieces of the mystery.

Police investigators follow a process similar to that used in **Clue**™. The investigators collect and evaluate evidence from a crime scene. All of the information they gather is compiled and placed in the criminal case file. As new evidence becomes available, it is added to the file.

Police investigators rarely learn about events in the same sequence in which they took place during the crime. Usually the leads are acquired in random order. Once a large portion of information is known, the police experts must sit down and put the pieces together, like you would assemble a jigsaw puzzle.

Deductive reasoning is the thought process that police investigators use to assemble the pieces of the criminal puzzle and reach a logical conclusion. In deductive reasoning, investigators utilize logical and critical-thinking skills to reach a conclusion.

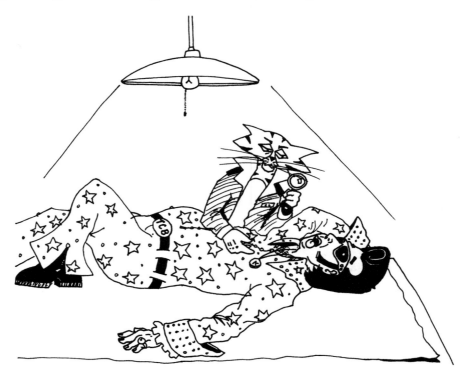

Crime Cat uses deductive reasoning to solve a crime by combining facts and evidence. This process is similar to piecing together the parts of a jigsaw puzzle until you form the whole.

Teacher Notes and Key for Lab 1-7, *The Deadly Picnic*

1. Students need about 50 minutes to complete this lab.
2. Explain to students how to make good use of the data tables provided in this lab. Encourage them to record vital information in these tables.

Data Tables and Conclusions

DATA TABLE 1

Question	Answer
Description of location where body was found	In the daisy field outside of Centerville
Approximate time and day of death	7:45 P.M. on Friday night, October 11
Weapon used to inflict fatal wound	Gun (one shot to the head)
Description of any footprints, tire prints, lip prints, etc., around the crime scene	Size 10 men and size 5 women shoes going from road to the crime site and size 5 returning from site back to the road Red lip print on wine glass Tire tracks belonging to deceased at road near site
Description of objects found at or around the crime scene	One cigarette butt Partially eaten chicken, potato salad, cake, and wine Wine glass had lipstick stain
Any other pieces of evidence that may help solve this crime	Yellow queen-size sheet under food

DATA TABLE 2

	Comments on size of women	Occupation and hobbies	City or place she lives	Medical information	Miscellaneous information
Rita		florist	lives west of town in country		father owns shooting range; she never wears lipstick
Lauren	over six feet tall	works at chemical supply house; used to play semi-professional basketball		allergic to all flowering plants	
Gail		school teacher; attends aerobics each Friday night at 7:30	lives in Jordan, a nearby town to Centerville		hates the color yellow; non-smoker
Janice	wears size 4 jeans	cosmetologist; teaches aerobics each Friday night at 7:30			hates yellow; nonsmoker
Peggy				allergic to grapes	never wears lipstick; room-mate of Elaine
Elaine	wears size 4 jeans	school teacher	lives in downtown Centerville		roommate of Peggy

Answers to Postlab Questions

1. Elaine

2. Answers will vary, but may include:

   ◆ *Rita:* never wears lipstick; lives in the country
   ◆ *Lauren:* has large feet; allergic to daisies
   ◆ *Gail:* hates yellow; at aerobics on Friday; nonsmoker
   ◆ *Janice:* teaches aerobics on Friday night; hates yellow; nonsmoker
   ◆ *Peggy:* allergic to grapes; never wears lipstick

3. Lives downtown; has small feet

4. Stories will vary. See example below:

   Elaine and Mr. Brooks had a date for a picnic on Friday night. Elaine volunteered to bring the sheet for the picnic if Mr. Brooks provided the food and wine. He picked up Elaine at about 6:00 P.M. They went to the picnic area out in the country. Elaine was jealous of Mr. Brooks's relationship with her roommate. She took a gun to the picnic for revenge.

   Elaine and Mr. Brooks walked down to the field of daisies and spread out their sheet for the food. They got everything out and began eating and drinking. Elaine took out the gun and shot Mr. Brooks in the head. She ran back up to the road where they left his car. She drove herself back to town and abandoned his car in a parking lot that was vacant. From here she walked a few blocks to her apartment.

Name _____ Date _____

THE DEADLY PICNIC
A Lab on Deductive Reasoning

Objective

You will use deductive reasoning to decide who committed the murder.

Background Information

Centerville police discovered the body of a 36-year-old white male (later identified as Gaven Brooks) in an open field of daisies about five miles outside of town. Mr. Brooks's body was discovered at 10:02 P.M. Friday night, October 11. He was found lying face up on a yellow, queen-size sheet. According to autopsy reports, one fatal gunshot to the back of the head ended Mr. Brooks's life. Scientists estimate that death occurred at about 7:45 P.M.

As investigators scanned the crime scene, they made the following notes:

◆ Paper plates filled with partially eaten fried chicken, potato salad, and chocolate cake were located near Mr. Brooks's body.

◆ An open bottle of red wine and two partially-filled glasses of wine were found next to the yellow sheet.

◆ One of the wine glasses had a smudge of red lipstick on the rim.

◆ A recently smoked cigarette butt was found near the sheet.

◆ Footprints from the road to the field were those of a male, size 10, and a female, size 5. The only footprints from the field back to the road were those of a female, size 5.

◆ Car tracks of the same wheel base and tread pattern as Mr. Brooks's automobile were found at the road. The car was not found at the scene.

◆ Later that evening Mr. Brooks's car was found abandoned in an empty parking lot in downtime Centerville.

Investigators believe that a female friend of Mr. Brooks was responsible for his demise. After questioning family and friends, it was discovered that the deceased had frequent social outings with six women who live in or near Centerville. The women's names are Rita, Lauren, Gail, Janice, Elaine, and Peggy.

In today's lab you will answer these questions: Who was responsible for the murder? What events surrounded this murder?

Materials

Pencil

Procedure

1. After reading the Background Information, record some important pieces of information in Data Table 1.

2. Read the special notes (given below) that the police gathered during their investigation. Record this information in Data Table 2.

3. Special notes gathered by police investigation:

   ◆ Janice works full time as a cosmetologist.

   ◆ Elaine and Gail are school teachers.

   ◆ Peggy and Elaine live together in a two-bedroom apartment in downtown Centerville.

   ◆ Gail lives in a nearby town called Jordan.

   ◆ Rita lives in a country house about three miles to the west of Centerville.

   ◆ Elaine and Janice are very petite women—they wear size 4 blue jeans.

   ◆ Gail and Janice are nonsmokers.

   ◆ Janice works part time as an aerobics instructor at a health club in Centerfield. She teaches a 7:30 P.M. step aerobics class each Friday night and has not missed a class in two years.

   ◆ Peggy is deathly allergic to grapes.

   ◆ Gail attends the aerobics class that Janice teaches. She has not missed a Friday night class in nine months.

   ◆ Lauren works at a chemical supply house.

   ◆ Rita's father owns a rifle range.

   ◆ Lauren is allergic to all species of flowering plants.

   ◆ Rita is a florist.

   ◆ Janice and Elaine have never met.

   ◆ Janice and Gail hate the color yellow.

   ◆ Lauren played center for a semi-professional basketball team five years ago. She has red hair and is 6-feet, 1-inch tall.

Postlab Questions

1. Who do you believe killed Mr. Brooks?

   _____

   _____

2. Cite key pieces of information that caused you to believe the other five women were innocent.

   _____

   _____

   _____

   _____

   _____

   _____

   _____

   _____

   _____

   _____

3. What information helped you identify the murderer?

   _____

   _____

4. On the back of this sheet, write a two-paragraph story that describes what you believe happened on the night of the murder. Explain how the couple got to the murder site, why they
   went there, what happened while they were there, and how the murderer escaped. What do
   you believe was her motive?

DATA TABLE 1

Question	Answer
Description of location where body was found	
Approximate time and day of death	
Weapon used to inflict fatal wound	
Description of any footprints, tire prints, lip prints, etc., around the crime scene	
Description of objects found at or around the crime scene	
Any other pieces of evidence that may help solve this crime	

DATA TABLE 2

	Comments on size of women	Occupation and hobbies	City or place she lives	Medical information	Miscellaneous information
Rita					
Lauren					
Gail					
Janice					
Peggy					
Elaine					

LESSON 1-8: I'VE GOT MY EYE ON YOU

A LESSON ON OBSERVING, REMEMBERING, AND RECORDING EVENTS

Crime scene investigators are trained to observe things carefully. During training they are encouraged to perceive the natural world through the use of all five of their senses. As soon as information is gathered, the investigators are taught to record it as precisely as possible.

Recorded information can take the form of notes or can be expressed in drawings and sketches. It should be both qualitative and quantitative. Qualitative information includes details such as hair color, eye color, color of clothing, and type of weapon displayed. Quantitative information includes numerical details such as the number of criminals or the height of the criminal.

Crime scene investigators are often asked to testify in court. When being questioned by the defense and prosecuting attorneys, the more facts and details the investigator can provide, the more likely it is that the case can be solved. If a witness's information is inadequate or flimsy, the criminal may be released.

Shoe and foot impressions left in soft earth are best preserved by photography and casting. Gypsum, a material used in dental work and the primary ingredient in plaster of Paris, is commonly used to make the casts. Liquified gypsum is poured into the impression and allowed to harden for 24 to 48 hours. Shoe and foot impressions from snow have even been recovered by spraying the impressions with a special wax-like material before pouring the gypsum. This material keeps the snowy impression intact so the gypsum can be poured and allowed to harden.

Figure 9. Shoe prints show characteristics such as tread, length, width, wear patterns, and this "S" logo.

One of a Kind

Shoe prints and impressions are unique because many things can affect the appearance of the sole of a shoe. (See Figure 9.) Length of wear, scuffs, and random marks can make the sole of a shoe unique. Once a cast is made of a shoe print, it is examined in the crime lab. Experts look for special identifying characteristics that make this print different from other prints. If police officers can recover the item suspected of making the print, comparisons can be made.

TEACHER NOTES AND KEY FOR LAB 1-8, *THAT'S MY STORY AND I'M STICKING TO IT!*

1. Students need 40 minutes on Day 1 and 30 minutes on Day 2 to complete this lab. Before the lab, make one photocopy of "Worksheet 1 for Lab 1-8." Divide the class into five groups. Cut the worksheet into five pieces and give one piece to each lab group. Remind each lab group not to tell other students what they will be doing on lab day. If they have trouble finding props, offer to help them. These students will role-play the scenario described in detail on their slip of paper.

2. As the assigned students role-play their crimes, the audience will record what they see on the Crime Report Sheets. Students cannot record information about the role-playing scenario in which they are involved.

3. Allow students to take their Crime Report Sheets home to study. On Day 2 they will use the notes they placed on their Crime Report Sheet to answer questions on "Worksheet 2 for Lab 1-8" about the five crimes. Be sure to have a copy of Worksheet 2 for *each student*.

Answers to Postlab Questions

1. Answers will vary.

2. You could not expect any three people to give the same account of a fight that they witnessed.

WORKSHEET 1 FOR LAB 1-8

Make one copy and cut into five strips. Give one strip to each lab group.

Crime #1

Two dark-haired boys; one girl

Both boys should wear baseball caps with logos and black shirts. They will be the criminals. One boy should have a dark-colored moustache. The crime will take place as the girl walks into the room with her pocketbook on her shoulder. One boy will come up to her from the audience and ask her what time it is. As she looks at her watch, the other boy will snatch her pocketbook from her arm. Both boys will quickly exit through the classroom door. The girl will yell: "Help! Someone stop them. They stole my purse."

Crime #2

One light-haired girl wearing a blue shirt, jeans, and tennis shoes; two boys

The girl is the criminal. Two boys will be in front of the room with their bank cards in their hands. They are waiting to use the teller machine to withdraw some cash. Boy 1 says, "I hate standing in line for this, plus my card sometimes will not even work." Boy 2 responds with, "I know what you mean!" The boy in front takes his cash and leaves. Boy 2 goes up to the machine and seems to be frustrated because he has trouble getting the card to work. Finally he gets his money and just as he removes it from the machine, the girl runs up behind him and puts a gun to his back. She says: "Your money or your life." He hands over the money, she strikes him on the head (lightly) with the gun. As he falls, she runs out the exit.

Crime #3

Two boys

Both are the criminals. They both have on a suit coat or blazer. One boy is sitting on a chair facing the front of the room. In his lap is a lunch box or bag. Inside is a ziplock bag full of a white powder. Boy 2 carries a bookbag or similar container. It is full of play money. He sits down next to Boy 1. Boy 1 opens his lunch box and pulls out the ziplock bag of white powder. Boy 2 opens the bag and touches his finger to the white powder and places a bit on his tongue. He nods his head, yes. Boy 2 opens the bookbag to reveal the money inside. He positions it so the audience can see the money. Boy 1 says: "It looks like a done deal." They exchange lunch bag and bookbag, then turn and walk away in opposite directions.

Crime #4

One boy; one girl

The boy has on a white shirt and a cap. He is the criminal. The girl has a key in her hand and appears to be opening her car door. The boy is crouched down on the other side of the car. As she gets the door open, he lunges around the car and pushes the girl into the front seat beside him. She yells: "Paul, what are you doing?" He responds: "I'll teach you to cheat on me." He places his hands around her neck and pretends to choke her. She struggles but eventually collapses. He closes the car door, cranks up the car, and drives away.

Crime #5

Two boys

Boy 1 is dressed in a white t-shirt and an apron. He is standing behind a cash register. Boy 2 has a dark-colored moustache and a jacket with pockets. Boy 2 enters the room with his hands in his jacket pocket. Boy 1 says: "Welcome to Joe's Diner. What can I fix for you, Sir?" Boy 2 raises his right hand, still inside his jacket pocket and says: "Quit your talking and give me all the money in the cash register or I'll shoot." Boy 1 removes cash from the register and hands it to the criminal. He takes it with his left hand and places it in his pocket. He tells Boy 1 to drop to the floor on his belly and place his hands over his head. As Boy 1 does this, Boy 2 runs out the door.

WORKSHEET 2 FOR LAB 1-8

Question number	Crime #1	Crime #2	Crime #3	Crime #4	Crime #5
1. Describe sex, hair color of each criminal.	Two males, both with dark hair	One female with light hair	Two males wearing suits	One male	One male
2. What color and type clothing did the criminal(s) wear?	Black	Blue shirt, jeans, tennis shoes		White t-shirt	Jacket
3. Did the criminal have a weapon? If so, describe it.	No	Gun	No	No	No, but appeared to have gun
4. Describe the crime and the place where it was committed.	Purse snatching; victim was outside	Money stolen at teller machine	Drugs sold on park bench	Female strangled in car	Robbery at Joe's Diner
5. Did you overhear any conversation during the crime?	Girl yelled for help and to stop them	"Your money or your life."	"It looks like a done deal."	"Paul, what are you doing?" "I'll teach you to cheat on me."	"Quit talking and give me all the money in the cash register or I'll shoot."
6. Describe any other features of the criminal.	One had moustache				Dark moustache; left-handed

Name _____ Date _____

That's My Story and I'm Sticking to It!
A Lab on Observing, Remembering, and Recording an Event

Objective

You will use your five senses to observe a simulated crime and then record in detail what you witnessed.

Background Information

Your job with the police department is to run a stake-out in an area that is plagued with a lot of crime. On this particular day, you conceal yourself in a location where you can witness criminal activities, but remain unseen. Your job is to observe any crimes and record both quantitatively and qualitatively what you witnessed.

You will be asked to answer a series of questions about the events you witness in lab today. If necessary, you may refer to your notes. The fate of the suspects rests on your testimony.

Materials

Pencil
Paper
Criminal acts (performed by your classmates)

Procedure, Day 1

1. Position yourself in an area where you can see the location where the crime will take place.

2. Place your pencil and Crime Report Sheet on the floor beside your desk or chair.

3. You and your classmates will enact five different crimes. Mentally record information as you witness each crime. Make use of your senses of sight and hearing during this process.

4. On the Crime Report Sheet and under Crime #1, record as much qualitative and quantitative detail as you can about the event you witnessed.

5. Repeat steps 1 through 4 for the other crimes you will observe.

6. Take this Crime Report Sheet home with you and study your notes. Think about what occurred. Did you accidentally omit any information? If so, add it at this time.

Procedure, Day 2

Use your notes about the crimes you observed yesterday to answer the questions on Worksheet 2.

Postlab Questions

1. Compare your answers with answers given by three other classmates. Of the five questions given on Worksheet 2, on how many did the four of you agree?

   _____

   _____

   _____

   _____

   _____

   _____

   _____

   _____

   _____

2. A witness is a person who observes an event. The testimony of witnesses can be very important to the outcome of a trial. If three witnesses were asked to testify about what they saw during a fight at school, would you expect all three to give the same information? Why or why not?

   _____

   _____

   _____

   _____

   _____

   _____

   _____

   _____

   _____

   _____

   _____

   _____

CRIME REPORT SHEET

Crime	Your observations
#1	
#2	
#3	
#4	
#5	

WORKSHEET 2 FOR LAB 1-8

Question number	Crime #1	Crime #2	Crime #3	Crime #4	Crime #5
1. Describe sex, hair color of each criminal.					
2. What color and type clothing did the criminal(s) wear?					
3. Did the criminal have a weapon? If so, describe it.					
4. Describe the crime and the place where it was committed.					
5. Did you overhear any conversation during the crime?					
6. Describe any other features of the criminals.					

SECTION 2

PHYSICAL SCIENCE LESSONS

LESSON 2-1: MAKING YOUR MARK
A LESSON ON TOOL MARKS

A tool mark is any impression, cut, or scratch caused by a tool on another object. For example, if you attempted to pry open a locked window with a screwdriver, the screwdriver would leave a tool mark on the window and windowsill.

Tool marks are most often found at burglary scenes where there was forced entry. These marks are actually impressions in wood or other material. Close examination of the impressions can reveal the size and shape of the tool. In some cases, scratches, nicks, and breaks on a tool can help an investigator individualize a particular mark and the tool used to make it.

Best Impressions

When feasible, investigators carry the material bearing a tool mark to the forensic lab. However, when this is not possible, they photograph the tool mark and make a cast of it. Investigators then test several types of tools to see if they can make a similar mark. By comparing the crime scene tool mark with several test tool marks, investigators can sometimes determine what kind of tool was used in the crime. If they are very lucky, they can use some unique characteristics of a tool, such as scratches or breaks, to identify it as the one used in the crime.

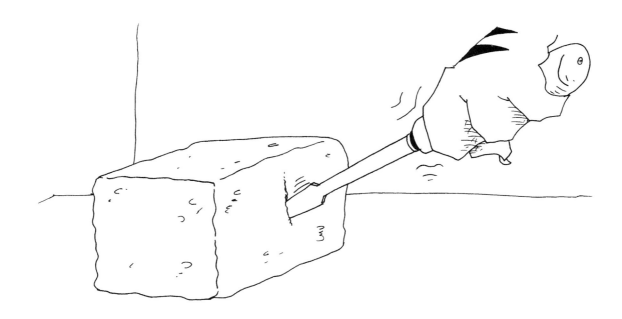

TEACHER NOTES AND KEY FOR LAB 2-1, TOOL MARKS THE SPOT

1. Students need 60 minutes to complete this activity.

2. Before the lab, collect ten screwdrivers that are very similar in size and shape. Label the screwdrivers with the letters A through J. Choose one of the screwdrivers to be the instrument used to break into Karen's house. For each lab group, make an impression of one side of this screwdriver in a small piece of clay, and label it "Crime Scene."

3. Results in the Data Table will vary, depending on the screwdrivers you used in this lab.

Answers to Postlab Qeustions

1. A tool mark is an impression, cut, or scratch caused by a tool on another object.

2. Yes, if the crime tool has very unique markings that were transferred to another object.

3. Yes. Answers will vary, depending on which screwdriver you used as the crime scene instrument.

4. Answers will vary, depending on the screwdriver you used. Hopefully, students could find ten points of comparison, such as striations in the metal, chips, bends, or worn places.

Name _____ Date _____

Tool Marks the Spot
A Lab on Tool Marks

Objective

You will use the dissecting microscope to examine several tool marks, and determine which tool was used to commit a crime.

Background Information

When Karen Jones arrives home, her back door is standing open. She approaches it slowly and notices that the door frame is badly damaged. It seems to Karen that the door has been forced open with a tool of some sort. Karen immediately turns around and goes to her neighbor's house to call the police.

When investigators arrive at Karen's, they enter the house and look around for anything suspicious. Then they ask Karen to check the house, and determine whether or not anything is missing. While waiting for Karen, the officers make a cast in plaster of Paris of the tool mark on the door frame. They can use the reconstructed tool cast to make a portable clay impression of the tool mark. After a quick tour of the premises, Karen reports that the only item absent is her stereo. It is the one she bought with her boyfriend last fall.

"Well," Karen says, "Ed used to live here, but he moved out several weeks ago. He took a carload of stuff with him. But he keeps calling me, asking for the stereo. I told him that I want to keep it and to stop calling! Maybe he's the one who broke in."

After getting Ed's address from Karen, the officers go to his house and ask him about the stereo. Ed denies breaking into Karen's home, and says that he does not have the stereo. He lets the officers look around his house and in his car, but they do not find it. However, they do find a tool box in Ed's trunk that contains several types of screwdrivers. With Ed's permission, they take the tool box to the forensic lab.

Materials

Clay
10 screwdrivers labeled A, B, C, D, E, F, G, H, I, J
Dissecting microscope
Notebook paper
Clay impression from crime scene
Ruler
Pencil

Procedure

1. Examine the clay impression from the crime scene under the dissecting microscope. Measure the width of the impression and record that width on the Data Table. Sketch the impression that you see in the clay—noting any special details—on the Data Table.

2. Roll out ten pieces of clay that are about 4 centimeters square. Place these clay squares on notebook paper, and label them as A through J. (See Figure 10.)

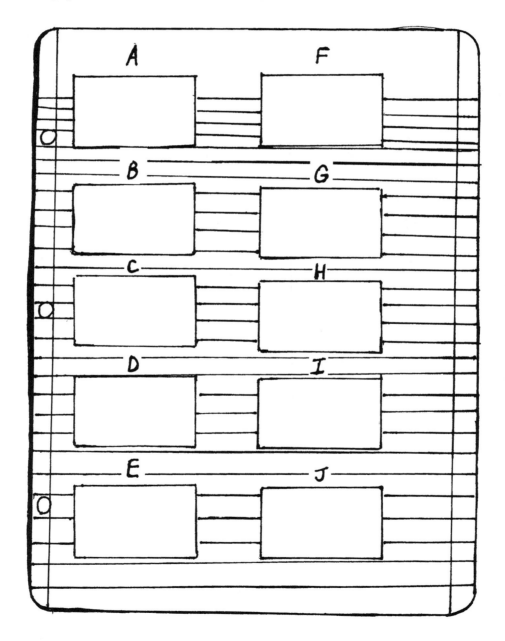

Figure 10. Place ten clay squares on notebook paper. Label the clay squares A through J.

3. In clay square A, make an impression of both sides of the tip of screwdriver A. Examine these impressions under the dissecting microscope. Measure the width of the impressions, and record these measurements on the Data Table. Sketch the impressions—noting any special details—on the Data Table.

4. Repeat step 3 for screwdrivers B through J in clay squares B through J.

5. Compare the sketch from the crime scene with sketches from screwdrivers A through J. If you can find five or more matching points on the crime scene sketch and one of the sketches A through J, you may have found the screwdriver used to break into Karen's house.

Postlab Questions

1. What is a tool mark?

   _____

   _____

2. Can investigators identify a specific tool that was used in a crime?

   _____

   _____

3. Did you find a screwdriver impression that matched the one from the crime scene? If so, which one?

   _____

   _____

4. How many matching points did you find between the clay impression of the crime scene screwdriver and the one most like it?

   _____

   _____

   _____

   _____

   _____

   _____

DATA TABLE

Sketches and measurements from the crime scene and from screwdrivers A through J.

Screwdrivers	Measurements	Sketch of impressions as seen under the dissecting microscope
A		
B		
C		
D		
E		
F		
G		
H		
I		
J		

LESSON 2-2: FORCES THAT FRACTURE GLASS
A LESSON ON EXAMINATION OF GLASS FRACTURES

Glass can provide valuable evidence about a crime. The comparisons possible with broken or fractured glass evidence include: physical match, probability of common origin, direction of impact, and sequence of impact. Physical match and probability of common origin of two or more pieces of glass can be determined by comparing the physical characteristics of glass samples. The penetration of glass by a high-speed projectile, such as a bullet, can leave evidence as to the direction of impact. If there is more than one hole in glass from flying projectiles, the sequence of their impact can be determined.

Straight and Circular Lines

When glass is penetrated by a projectile, it fractures in two ways: radially and concentrically. A radial crack is a straight line that extends from the point of impact. A concentric crack or fracture is a circular line of broken glass around the point of impact.

When a high-speed projectile hits glass, it bends the glass as far as possible, then breaks it. In Figure 11: (a) The first fractures appear on the surface opposite that of the force. These first fractures develop into radial lines. (b) The continued motion of the projectile through the glass puts tension on the front surface of the glass, causing concentric fractures.

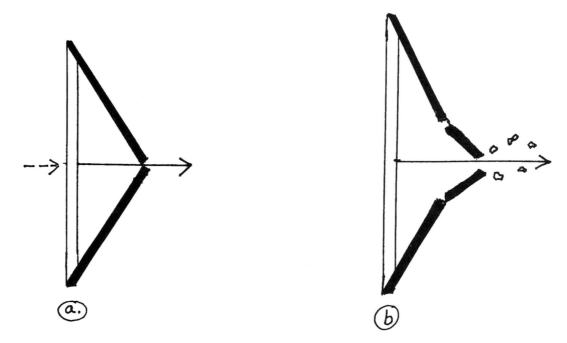

Figure 11.

Bullet Holes

When a high-speed projectile, such as a bullet, penetrates glass, it leaves an exit hole that is larger than its entrance hole. This helps the investigator determine the direction of impact. The hole produced is often crater-shaped, and surrounded by concentric and radial fractures.

A piece of glass may be penetrated by more than one projectile. It is possible to determine the order in which the penetrations occurred by examining the fracture lines. A new fracture line will always stop when it reaches an existing fracture (see Figure 12). Therefore, fracture lines from the first penetration will not end at any other fracture lines.

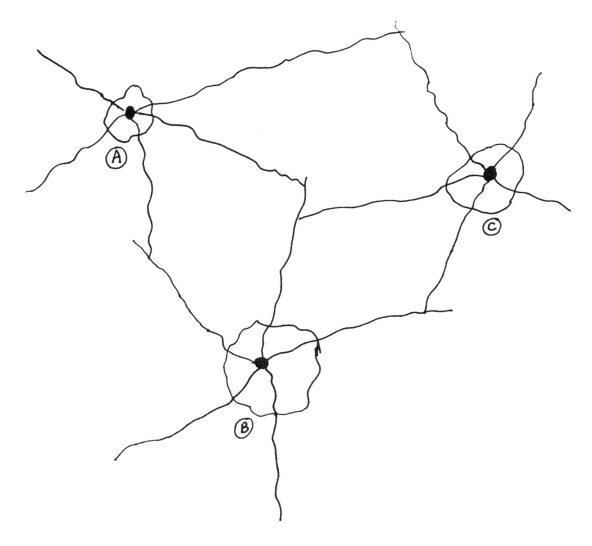

Figure 12. The sequence in which these bullet holes penetrated this glass can be determined by examining the fracture lines. In this case, bullet hole B was first, C was second, and A was third.

Teacher Notes and Key for Lab 2-2, Glass Is Breaking Up

1. Students need 30 minutes to complete this activity.

2. Prepare a piece of window glass for each lab group or one for the entire class to share. On one side of each piece of glass, tape the word "inside" so that students will know that this was inside the house. At a target range, or some other safe location, shoot three BB's or pellets through the pieces of window glass:

   a. The first shot (A) should be from the inside.

   b. The second (C) and third (B) shots should be from the outside.

Answers to Data Table

	Fired from inside of the house	*Fired from outside of the house*	*Order in which this bullet hole was created (1st, 2nd, or 3rd)*
Bullet hole A	yes	no	1st
Bullet hole B	no	yes	3rd
Bullet hole C	no	yes	2nd

Answers to Postlab Questions

1. Yes. The first hole was made by a gun fired inside the house.

2. Hole A. It was made by a bullet leaving the house. The diameter of the hole is larger on the outside where the bullet exited than it is on the inside where the bullet entered.

3. No. Evidence suggests that Mr. Hubbard fired the first shot.

4. Answers will vary. Students might write a story suggesting that Mr. Hubbard saw prowlers in the back yard and fired at them through the window. Or, they might write that the firing of Mr. Hubbard's gun was accidental, but it alarmed someone who fired back.

Name _____ Date _____

Glass Is Breaking Up
A Lab on Examination of Glass Fractures

Objective

You will examine several pieces of fractured glass to determine the direction of force and the sequence in which the fractures occurred.

Background Information

It's late, and Mr. and Mrs. Hubbard are in the kitchen getting a bedtime snack. They are still discussing the rise of violence in their neighborhood, and the fear this violence has caused. Neighborhood violence is a topic they have discussed daily, and with good reason. The increase in burglaries and assaults in their part of town has been alarming.

"Try not to worry all the time, Martha," Mr. Hubbard is saying. "You know that I've put new locks on all the doors, and I have bought a gun for every room. Remember, there is one on the top of the refrigerator."

"Of course I remember. As a matter of fact, I wish I could forget that we have a house full of guns. You know that I don't like them, and I don't want them in our home. We've been over this issue a thousand times, and you are still buying guns."

"I feel like we need a little extra protection right now. I hope this violence will come to an end, but no one can guarantee it. I don't want us to be defenseless."

"And I don't want us to accidentally shoot each other. I'm taking my ice cream and book up to bed to read for a while." Mrs. Hubbard pauses and looks back at her husband. "Can you at least promise me that you won't use these guns?"

"Well, Martha, I can't do that. But I will promise to *try* not to use them. I'll only pull one out in an emergency."

Martha heads upstairs, but freezes on the top landing when she hears three gunshots in quick succession. She drops her bowl and races down the stairs to find Mr. Hubbard standing in the kitchen, gun in one hand and spoon in the other. There are three bullet holes in the window.

Materials

Window glass containing three bullet holes
Hand lens
Labels
Rulers

Procedure

1. Examine the window and the bullet holes in it. Notice that one side of the window is marked "inside."

2. Label the holes as A, B, and C. Avoid covering any fracture lines with your labels.

3. By examining the shape of the bullet holes and the width of their entrance and exit paths, determine whether the bullets were fired from the outside of the house toward the inside, or from the inside to the outside. Enter this information on the Data Table.

4. Examine the fracture lines. Determine which bullet hole was created first. Remember, none of the fracture lines from the first hole will end at another fracture line. Enter this information on the Data Table.

5. Determine the sequence in which the other two bullet holes were formed. Enter this on the Data Table.

DATA TABLE

Direction from which bullets were fired and the sequence in which bullet holes were formed.

	Fired from inside of the house	*Fired from outside of the house*	*Order in which this bullet hole was created (1st, 2nd, or 3rd)*
Bullet hole A			
Bullet hole B			
Bullet hole C			

Postlab Questions

1. Do you think that Mr. Hubbard shot his gun? Why?

   _____

   _____

   _____

   _____

2. Which bullet hole was created first: A, B, or C? Was this hole made by a bullet entering the house or by a bullet leaving the house? How do you know?

   _____

   _____

   _____

   _____

3. When Mrs. Hubbard came downstairs, the first thing she asked her husband was, "What happened?" Mr. Hubbard told her that someone had taken three shots at him. Do you think his story is true? Why or why not?

   _____

   _____

   _____

   _____

4. Based on your lab results, write an end to the scenario presented in the Background Information.

   _____

   _____

   _____

   _____

   _____

   _____

   _____

LESSON 2-3: GLASS CHIP TIPS
A LESSON ON GLASS IDENTIFICATION

Glass fragments can be used as evidence to help place a suspect at the scene of a crime. Because different kinds of glass have different physical characteristics, types of glass can be distinguished from one another. For example, chips of glass from a broken window may fall into a perpetrator's trouser cuff or shoes. A forensic scientist can identify these chips as part of the broken window. Similarly, parts of a broken headlight found at the scene of a hit-and-run can be used to identify the suspected vehicle.

Composition of Glass

Glass is a hard, brittle substance made of silicon oxides (sand), lime, soda, and oxides of metals. The metal oxides found in most window glass are sodium, calcium, magnesium, and aluminum. Automobile headlights and other heat-resistant types of glass, such as Pyrex®, contain boron oxides.

Safety Glass

Broken glass can be sharp and dangerous. That is why automobile manufacturers use tempered and safety glass in vehicles. Tempered glass is made strong by a rapid heating-and-cooling process that introduces stress to the glass surface. When tempered glass breaks, it fragments into small squares that do not have sharp edges. Therefore, tempered glass is not so dangerous as other types of glass. It is used in the side and rear windows of cars and trucks. Windshields are made of laminated or safety glass. This type of glass is strong and break resistant because it is made by sandwiching a layer of plastic between two pieces of ordinary window glass.

Different Densities for Different Glass

The forensic scientist uses the physical properties of glass to associate one type of glass fragment with another. One of these physical properties is density. Because different types of glass contain different combinations of metal oxides, they have different densities. Density refers to a material's mass per unit volume, and can be summarized in the formula:

$$\text{Density} = \frac{\text{Mass}}{\text{Volume}}$$

The density of a substance remains constant, no matter what the size of the substance. Thus, density of glass can be used to help identify it. A simple three-step method for determining density of a sample is:

1. Weigh the sample to find its mass.
2. Determine the volume of the sample.
3. Divide the mass of the sample by its volume.

See Figure 13.

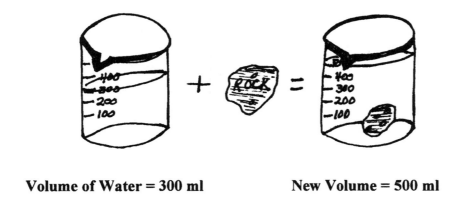

Volume of Water = 300 ml   **New Volume = 500 ml**

Volume of Rock	=	New Volume of Water	−	Original Volume of Water
200 ml	=	500 ml	−	300 ml

Figure 13. To determine volume by water displacement, place a known amount of water in a container. Add the substance whose volume you want to know, then read the new volume. The difference between the original and the new volume is equal to the volume of that substance.

TEACHER NOTES AND KEY FOR LAB 2-3, GLASS CAN TELL ON YOU

1. Students need 30 minutes to complete this activity.

2. You will need five types of glass fragments. Sources of glass fragments might include junk yards, glass recycling bins, and auto glass repair shops. When possible, select rounded pieces of glass.

3. Before the lab, decide which glass fragment sample (A, B, C, D, or E) will match the glass found at the scene of the hit-and-run accident. This sample will be the same as the accident sample.

4. Because glass is not very dense, students may need to use several pieces to see a change in volume in the graduated cylinder. Be sure they determine the mass of all the glass pieces they used to find volume.

5. Results on the Data Table will depend on what glass samples you use.

Answers to Postlab Questions

1. The answer depends on which glass sample you decided to use as the glass found at the scene of the accident.

Type of Glass	*Density*
Porcelain	2.3-2.5 g/ml
Window	2.47-2.56 g/ml
Headlight	2.47-2.63 g/ml

2. Glass is denser than water because it sinks in water. Therefore, the density of glass must be more than 1 g/ml.

3. No. The evidence from this experiment *suggests* that this suspect hit Brian's car. All cars of the same make and model will have headlight glass of the same density.

4. When determining density, it does not matter what size sample you use. However, you must use the same size sample to determine volume and mass.

Name _____ Date _____

Glass Can Tell on You
A Lab on Glass Identification

Objectives

You will determine the densities of several glass samples.

You will determine whether or not two glass samples originated from the same piece.

Background Information

Brian is admiring his new car from the front porch of his house. It is parked on the street behind his mother's car. Brian and his friend Ned are resting after a morning of vacuuming, washing, and waxing this prized possession.

"It sure is a beauty," Ned agrees, nodding his head while taking the last bite of a peanut butter and jelly sandwich. "That wax job did the trick. Everything on it shines like new."

Brian's "new" car is new to him, and he is very proud of it. By working at the Corner Shoppette for the last two years, he was able to save enough money to buy this beauty and pay for its insurance. It has been hard work, but he's pleased with his accomplishments.

Brian and Ned rise to go into the house for soft drinks when they hear the screech of metal against metal. In disbelief, they turn around in time to see a car racing away from them down the street. Brian's beautiful new car is still bouncing from the impact of the run-away vehicle. Both boys race to the car and stare at it in shock.

No longer a beautiful car, Ned's pride and joy has a crushed left rear fender and quarter panel. Its left rear door is hanging open at an odd angle. Glass is laying all over the street. Brian feels like crying.

"Oh no, Ned, look at my car! It's ruined! I cannot believe this guy just hit me and kept going." In Ned's opinion, Brian may be right about the car. It looks terrible.

"Hurry, let's call the police. Maybe they can catch the guy before he gets too far," Ned suggests.

When the police arrive, they find Brian and Ned sitting sadly beside the wrecked car. The police question the boys and find that they did not see much. All they know is that the car that hit Brian's parked vehicle was large and beige. Finally, the investigating officers examine the wrecked car, photograph it from every angle, then start taking samples of broken glass from the road.

"Hey, what are you doing?" Brian asks. It seems to him that enough has happened to his car without the police taking away any more of it.

"We need these to positively identify the vehicle that hit your car. Some of this glass may have come from his headlights. As soon as we have a suspect, and some results from the forensic lab, we'll give you a call."

Materials

Glass sample taken from the road beside Brian's car

5 suspect glass samples taken from broken headlights of long, beige cars (Samples A, B, C, D, E) (**Caution:** Sharp glass can cause cuts!)

Graduated cylinder

Scale or triple-beam balance

Tweezers

Water

Paper towels

Procedure

1. Place the glass sample from Brian's car on a scale and determine its mass in grams. Record this mass on the Data Table.

2. Remove this sample from the scale. Repeat step 1 with the five suspect glass samples.

3. Place 20 milliliters of water in the graduated cylinder. Then add the glass sample taken from Brian's car to the water in the graduated cylinder. Read the new volume on the cylinder in milliliters and record it on the Data Table.

4. Remove this sample from the graduated cylinder. Repeat step 3 with the five suspect glass samples.

5. Calculate the volume of the glass by subtracting Column 1 from Column 2.

6. Divide the volume of each sample by its mass to determine that sample's density. Record the densities for the glass from Brian's car and from the five suspect cars on the Data Table.

© 1998 by The Center for Applied Research in Education

DATA TABLE

Density of glass from Brian's car and from five suspect cars.

	1. Original volume in graduated cylinder	2. Volume after glass sample was added	3. Subtract Column 1 from Column 2 to find volume of sample	4. Mass of sample	5. Density of sample
Brian's car	20 ml				
Suspect A	20 ml				
Suspect B	20 ml				
Suspect C	20 ml				
Suspect D	20 ml				
Suspect E	20 ml				

Postlab Questions

1. From your experimental results, which suspect glass sample matched the glass found at the scene of the hit-and-run accident?

   _____

   _____

2. Water has a density of 1 g/ml. Based on your work, does glass have a density greater than 1 g/ml or less than 1 g/ml? Explain your answer.

   _____

   _____

   _____

   _____

   _____

   _____

3. Does the evidence from this experiment positively prove that this suspect hit Brian's car? Explain your answer.

   _____

   _____

   _____

   _____

   _____

   _____

4. All of the glass samples you tested were not the same size. When determining density, does the size of the sample make a difference? Why or why not?

   _____

   _____

   _____

   _____

   _____

   _____

LESSON 2-4: UNKNOWN SUBSTANCES
A LESSON ON STANDARDIZED TESTS USED TO IDENTIFY UNKNOWN SUBSTANCES

The collection of evidence at a crime scene is very important to any criminal investigation. Once this evidence has been collected and packaged properly, it is transported to the crime lab.

Crime labs frequently receive unknown substances taken from a crime scene. Experts in the crime lab have the task of determining the physical and chemical identity of these substances. Many times these mysterious substances are illegal drugs. The findings of the crime lab are important in determining the guilt or innocence of a suspect.

Give the Sample a Test

In the case of determining the identity of an unknown substance, crime lab experts must use testing procedures that give characteristic results. These tests and their results must be established prior to the examination of the unknown substance. Once the tests are verified, they are recorded and used repeatedly to prove the identity of suspect substances. For example, if you want to determine if an unknown white powder is cocaine, you must have a previously established, positive test for cocaine. Then you can conduct this established test on an unknown white powder.

The More the Merrier

It is also important to perform more than one positive test on an unknown. Proper identification requires that you use enough different tests to rule out the possibility that the unknown may be any other substance. For example, a lab technician may be testing an unknown white powder to determine whether or not it is cocaine. To be thorough, this technician will run a series of tests on the powder. If all tests are positive for cocaine, then the technician feels certain that the results are correct.

The forensic scientist in the crime lab must carefully perform each test on the unknown. Then test results must be precisely recorded. The results he or she gathers must be so exact that the identification is correct beyond any reasonable doubt.

TEACHER NOTES AND KEY FOR LAB 2-4, WHITE POWDERS

1. This lab requires 50 minutes.

2. Lugol's solution is iodine solution. Dilute acetic acid is vinegar.

3. Prepare 1M (Molar) sodium carbonate by adding 53 grams of sodium carbonate powder to 500 ml of distilled water. When it combines with calcium chloride solution, a precipitate of calcium carbonate will form.

4. Do not tell students the actual identity of the substances you are using to represent the illegal drugs. After the lab you may wish to discuss precipitates, positive Lugol's test for starch, and the reaction of sodium bicarbonate and vinegar to produce carbon dioxide bubbles.

5. Use the following substances for the six white powders:

   A—Baking soda
   B—Calcium chloride
   C—Corn starch
   D—Plaster of paris
   E—Table sugar
   F—Table salt

6. Prepare small ziplock bags with about 1/4 cup of each of the six substances. Label the bags with the proper letters. Prepare enough bags so each lab group will have six different bags.

7. For Part B, select a different substance for each lab group and place it in a small plastic bag. Write a number on each bag that represents the locker number in which the substance was found. Keep a record of what numbers match which substances. For example: place 1/2 cup of calcium chloride in bag labeled #12, or place 1/2 cup of plaster of paris in bag labeled #44.

ANTICIPATED RESULTS FOR DATA TABLE 1

Name of known substance	Observation with hand lens	Addition of acetic acid	Hot plate results	Addition of water	Addition of sodium carbonate	Addition of Lugol's solution
A—Brogaine	ND	bubbles	ND	ND	ND	ND
B—Speclate	crystals	ND	ND	dissolves	white powder forms	ND
C—Rotaran	ND	ND	ND	ND	ND	turns black
D—Barrop	powder	ND	ND	ND—will harden over time; does not dissolve	ND	ND
E—Lixonin	ND	turns brown; burns	ND	ND	ND	ND
F—Table salt	crystals	ND	ND	dissolves	ND	ND

Answers to Postlab Questions

1. Answers will vary, but may include:

   A — bubbles when combined with acetic acid

   B — forms a solid when combined with sodium carbonate

   C — reacts with Lugol's to turn brown

   D — does not dissolve in water; hardens over time

   E — burns when heated

   F — individual grains look very much alike

2. Answers will vary depending on the unknown given the group. Anything but table salt will be an illegal drug.

3. The findings of the crime lab will determine the innocence or the guilt of a suspect.

4. You had to establish a set of standards or characteristics for comparison.

Name _____ Date _____

White Powders

A Lab on Standardized Tests
Used to Identify Unknown Substances

Objectives

You will perform a series of tests to determine the physical and chemical characteristics of several unknown powders.

You will utilize your test results to identify an unknown substance.

Background Information

Jackson High School has a drug problem. Over the past year, illegal drugs have been seized from student lockers on five occasions. All of these illegal drugs are white powders that look remarkably like table salt. During a recent locker search, investigators collected several ziplock bags filled with a white powder. Before charges can be pressed on the individual in possession, the identity of the powders must be established.

You are a member of a forensic science lab team that has been sent to Jackson High School. A temporary lab facility has been prepared at the high school. The unknown white powders are delivered to you in the lab so you can determine their identity.

Due to limitations in equipment at the school, you have been asked to use a simple series of tests to determine the identity of the powders. To enable you to do this, six known white powders have been provided. You will run tests on each of the six known powders and record your results. Later you will compare results with those from tests of unknown powders collected during locker seizures. Your findings will determine the charges (if any) brought against the students in possession of drugs.

A brief overview of the white powders previously discovered at Jackson High School includes the following:

Brogaine—a mild hallucinogen. First offense is usually probation.

Speclate—a mild stimulant; often results in psychological dependence. First offense results in 6 months to 1 year in prison.

Rotaran—a strong stimulant; causes physical dependence. First offense results in 1 year to 3 years in prison.

Barrop—a moderate depressant; causes physical dependence. First offense results in 1 year to 3 years in prison.

Lixonin—a strong narcotic that causes physical and psychological dependence. First offense can result in 5 to 10 years in prison.

Table salt—this was found in one student's locker as a joke.

© 1998 by The Center for Applied Research in Education

Materials

Samples of the six white powders (A, B, C, D, E, F) in individual ziplock plastic bags:

A — Brogaine
B — Speclate
C — Rotaran
D — Barrop
E — Lixonin
F — Table salt

Teaspoon

Hand lens

Black construction paper

Aluminum foil

Hot plates

Labels

Lugol's solution

Medicine dropper

Dilute acetic acid

Distilled water

1M (Molar) sodium carbonate solution

7 test tubes and stoppers

Stirring rod

Unknown sample in a ziplock bag

Procedure, Part A:
Developing a positive test for the six known powders

Obtain a ziplock bag of each of the six known samples A through F. Record your results for tests conducted on the six known powders in Data Table 1. If nothing happens in a specific test on a known substance, record ND (no data) in the proper location on the data table. At the end of Part A, you should have something written in each box on the chart.

1. Place a small amount of sample A on the black paper and observe its appearance with a hand lens. Record your results. Repeat this for samples B through F. Dispose of the samples and the paper in the waste disposal can.

2. Place 1/2 teaspoon of sample A in a test tube. Add 10 drops of vinegar to the test tube. Record your observations. Repeat this test with the remaining five powders. Wash out each test tube.

3. Label the six pieces of aluminum foil with A, B, C, D, E, F. Place 1/2 teaspoon of each of the six samples on the appropriate piece of foil. Place the six squares of foil on a hot plate set at a medium setting. Observe each for several minutes. Record your results. Dispose of the foil and contents.

4. Place 1/2 teaspoon of sample A in a test tube. Add 10 ml of distilled water. Stopper the test tube and shake for a few seconds. Record your observations. Repeat this for the remaining samples. Do not dispose of these samples. You will use them in the next step.

5. Using the six test tubes from step 4, add 5 ml of sodium carbonate solution to each test tube. Observe and record what occurs in each test tube. Wash out the test tubes.

6. Place 1/2 teaspoon of each sample in a clean test tube. Add 10 drops of Lugol's solution to each test tube. Record your results. Wash out the test tubes.

DATA TABLE 1

Observations from tests done on white powders.

Name of known substance	Observation with hand lens	Addition of acetic acid	Hot plate results	Addition of water	Addition of sodium carbonate	Addition of Lugol's solution
A—Brogaine						
B—Speclate						
C—Rotaran						
D—Barrop						
E—Lixonin						
F—Table salt						

Procedure, Part B:
Identification of unknown substance

You now have the test results for each white powder on Data Table 1. These results will help you to determine the identity of an unknown substance by comparison. Several unknown substances were discovered in student lockers today. Different forensic teams have been asked to identify some of the unknowns. In Data Table 2, write down the number of the ziplock bag whose contents you will analyze. This number indicates the locker from which the baggie was taken. Compare your results with those in Data Table 1 to determine what substance the student had in his or her locker. Be careful; your results will determine whether or not charges should be pressed against the student.

1. Write down the locker number on the bag in Data Table 2.

2. Perform all the tests you performed in Part A on this unknown substance. Record your findings on Data Table 2.

3. Compare the results in Data Table 2 with the results in Data Table 1.

DATA TABLE 2

Reaction of powders to chemical tests.

	Hand lens observation	*Addition of acetic acid*	*Hot plate results*	*Addition of water*	*Addition of sodium carbonate*	*Addition of Lugol's solution*
Unknown sample #_____						

Postlab Questions

1. Describe one positive test from Data Table 1 for each of the six powders.

   _____
   _____
   _____

2. Was the powder you examined in Part B one of the illegal drugs or was it table salt? Explain how you arrived at this conclusion.

   _____
   _____
   _____

3. Explain why forensic scientists must be very accurate when examining substances in the laboratory.

   _____
   _____
   _____

4. Explain why Part A was a vital part of this experiment.

   _____
   _____
   _____

LESSON 2-5: PRINT PATTERNS
A LESSON ON IDENTIFICATION OF FINGERPRINTS

Since 1901, fingerprinting has been used as a method of positively identifying individuals. Because no two people have the same fingerprints, a good print can help solve a crime.

Fingerprints are impressions created by ridges on the skin. On the tips of fingers, palms of hands, and soles of feet, the skin has tiny ridges that provide traction to help us grip things. Everyone has a unique pattern of skin ridges. These ridges form before a baby is born, and maintain their pattern throughout life. As you grow, the pattern gets larger, but it does not change.

Skin Deep

Skin is made of two distinct layers: the dermis and the epidermis. The dermis, which is the deepest layer, contains sweat glands, oil glands, nerves, and blood vessels. Above the dermis, the epidermis is made of several layers of cells that are arranged along ridge patterns. The outer-most cells of the epidermis are dead and they generally dry out and fall off.

Lots of Latents

When a person touches an object, the perspiration, oils, and amino acids on his or her skin are transferred to that object. Sometimes an impression of the ridge pattern is left in the deposit. This impression is called a *fingerprint*. Such prints are usually not visible to the naked eye, so they are called *latent*, or hidden, prints.

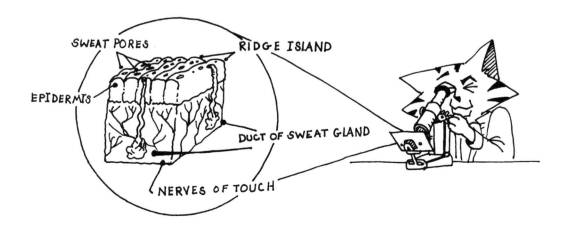

Do You Loop, Whorl, or Arch?

Fingerprints have general patterns of ridges that allow them to be classified and compared. All fingerprints are divided into three large groups, based on their ridge pattern:

a. *loops* are found in 65% of the population

b. *whorls* are found in 35% of the population

c. *arches* are found in 5% of the population

  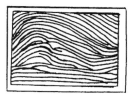

Save the Prints

Latent fingerprints at a crime scene must be located and preserved. There are two basic techniques for finding fingerprints: dusting and chemically fixing.

◆ Hard surfaces such as glass and tile yield prints when lightly dusted with powder. Fingerprint powders come in a variety of colors so that the investigator can always apply one that will contrast with the surface holding the print. The powders can be brushed in place with either a camel-hair or fiberglass brush.

◆ Chemicals can be used to help find fingerprints on many types of smooth surfaces. Iodine was the first chemical used by investigators to develop fingerprints. When solid iodine is heated, it produces a purple vapor that interacts with a component of the fingerprint to reveal a print. The print begins to fade as soon as iodine fuming stops. To preserve it, the print can be photographed. Or, it can be sprayed with starch to create a purple print that will last several weeks or months.

Another chemical used to visualize fingerprints is ninhydrin. Ninhydrin reacts with amino acids in the print to form a blue-purple color. Most prints are visible within two to four hours after spraying with ninhydrin.

Silver nitrate makes prints on many surfaces visible. Some of the residue in a print is salt, or sodium chloride. The chloride ion of salt will react with silver nitrate to produce silver chloride. Silver chloride is colorless, but can be seen with an ultraviolet light as a black or reddish-brown color.

Super Glue® fuming produces good prints on nonporous surfaces such as metal, leather, and plastic. In this technique, Super Glue® is heated in an enclosed area that contains the evidence in question. Prints appear in an off-white shade.

Teacher Notes and Key for Lab 2-5, *Pointing Out Perpetrators*

1. This lab requires about 80 minutes.

2. Before lab day, prepare the aquarium for Super Glue® fuming. In a large, clean aquarium, place a light bulb or small lamp that will fit inside of one-half of an aluminum can. Cut a piece of plywood or stiff cardboard to act as a cover for the aquarium. **CAUTION:** Do not breathe fumes.

3. Wearing rubber gloves, distribute clean glass slides to all students for them to touch. Students should label the slides with their names. Collect the students' slides, remove the names from these slides, and then label them as slides A, B, C, D, E, F, G, H. Place them inside the aquarium for fuming during lab. To fume, drop a little Super Glue® on the can. Cover the aquarium and turn on the light bulb. You will begin to see white prints form on the slides in about 15 minutes.

4. When prints are visible, remove the slides, holding them by the edges to protect the prints. Place the slides in front of the room. Students can view these slides to identify the party conspirators.

Answers to Postlab Questions

1. Answers will vary.

2. Answers will vary. The most common type of fingerprint is the loop.

3. Crime scene technicians collect fingerprints in an effort to identify everyone who was present at the crime scene.

4. In case of kidnapping, a child could be identified and returned to his or her parents.

Name _____ Date _____

Pointing Out Perpetrators
A Lab on Identification of Fingerprints

Objectives

You will collect and preserve fingerprints.
You will analyze and identify fingerprints.

Background Information

When Mr. Crowe walked into his science class, he was surprised by a birthday cake topped with an incredible number of candles. Students broke into an off-key rendition of "Happy Birthday" and gave him a standing ovation.

"For the first time, I'm speechless," Mr. Crowe said. "I can't believe you guys prepared this birthday surprise for me. Do you really think I need all of those candles?! Before we eat, tell me who brought the cake, dishes, forks, napkins, and drinks? I want to thank you personally."

No one spoke as Mr. Crowe looked around the room, waiting for a response. "What's the matter? Are you bashful? Who brought all of this good stuff?"

Still the students smiled and remained silent. Mr. Crowe was amused, and decided to make the best of the situation. "OK, let's try something. The birthday party conspirators moved some glass slides from the table to set up the cake. I think we can use these slides to identify our modest hosts."

Materials

Glass slides with fingerprints of each student
Rubber gloves
1 large aquarium
1 12-ounce aluminum can, top half removed
60-volt light bulb
Light socket and cord
Super Glue®
Piece of plywood large enough to cover aquarium
Forceps
Paper towels
Clean white paper
Transparent tape
Pencil and paper
Tape or labels

Procedure

1. Your teacher has set up a large aquarium for Super Glue® fuming. The aquarium is equipped with a light bulb inside an aluminum can to heat the Super Glue®. Fumes from the glue "fix" the invisible fingerprints on the slide so that they can be seen. Several sets of the "Party Conspirators" prints have been found on glass slides. The slides have been placed in the aquarium, where they must remain for 15 minutes. **CAUTION:** Do not breathe fumes.

2. Make a fingerprint identification sheet of everyone in your class.

   a. Turn a pencil sideways and rub a thick spot of graphite on your paper with your pencil.

   b. Place your right forefinger in the graphite, rolling it firmly from right to left.

   c. Hold up your right index finger so that your lab partner can place a strip of clear tape on the graphite.

   d. Then gently remove the tape and stick it to a sheet of white paper.

   e. Label this print with your name.

   f. Repeat steps *a* through *e* for everyone in your class so that your paper has a sample of everyone's right index fingerprint.

3. Remove one of the glass slides from the aquarium. A print should be visible on the slide. Be careful not to smear or destroy the print.

4. Compare the print on the slide to the set of prints you have taken from the class.

5. When you find a match, write the name of the conspirator on the next sheet.

6. Also describe on the next sheet each conspirator's print as a loop, whorl, or arch.

7. Examine the prints of your classmates and classify them as loops, whorls, or arches.

8. Determine the percentage of loops, the percentage of whorls, and the percentage of arches in the class and enter that information on the Data Table. To find percentage, divide the total number of students into the number of students with that type of print.

Names of party conspirators _____

_____

_____

Types of prints _____

_____

_____

DATA TABLE

Number of students in class with loops, whorls, and arches.

	Loops	*Whorls*	*Arches*
Number of students			
Percentage of students			

Postlab Questions

1. What was the most common type of fingerprint in your class?

   _____

   _____

2. Are the percentages of students with each type of print similar to the worldwide percentages?

   _____

   _____

3. Why do crime scene technicians collect fingerprints?

   _____

   _____

   _____

   _____

4. What are some reasons a parent might want to have his or her child fingerprinted?

   _____

   _____

   _____

LESSON 2-6: FALLING BLOOD DROPS
A LESSON ON BLOOD-DROP ANALYSIS

The patterns left by falling or projected drops of blood can help investigators determine where a crime took place. Therefore, blood drops and stains should be examined closely before the evidence is collected.

Shapely Drops

The shape of a blood drop can indicate the distance from which the blood fell and the angle of its impact. However, very few studies have been done on the patterns produced when blood impacts a surface. Therefore, a thorough forensic scientist will carry out his or her own experiments on the shape of blood droplets. To be accurate, this scientist will conduct the tests under conditions very much like those found at the crime scene.

While a droplet is falling, it is primarily spherical in shape. This is surprising to some people, who may have visualized droplets as tear shaped, as cartoonists often draw them. The smaller a drop, the more spherical its shape during a fall.

Drop Acceleration

As a drop falls through the air, it accelerates until it reaches a constant or terminal velocity. Measurements have shown that a blood drop, resulting from dripping at a height of 15 feet, has a volume of about 0.05 ml and falls at a velocity of about 25 feet per second. Smaller drops have a terminal velocity that is less than 25 feet per second, and larger drops have a terminal velocity that is greater than 25 feet per second. Therefore, an individual blood droplet can give an investigator the following useful information:

a. the droplet's speed at time of impact,
b. the direction of the droplet's travel, and
c. the approximate size of the blood drop.

Round Drops

If you examine a blood droplet that struck a surface straight-on (at a 90-degree angle from the surface), the droplet is generally round. Straight-on impacts on hard, smooth surfaces produce round droplets with smooth edges. Higher velocities and rougher surfaces produce drops with more ragged edges (see Figure 14).

Figure 14. Drops that have ragged edges have fallen at high velocities.

Elongated Drops

The angle of impact of a droplet affects the droplet's shape. As we have said, when the angle of impact is 90 degrees, the droplet is round. However, droplets that fall on surfaces at an angle that is greater than 90 degrees have elongated shapes. The larger the angle, the more elliptical the droplet (see Figure 15).

Figure 15. Droplets that fall on surfaces at angles greater than 90 degrees form elliptical patterns.

Dripping and Spraying

Blood drops can be produced in several ways. A droplet that forms slowly, as in a dripping wound, has a volume of about 0.05 ml. However, smaller droplets are produced during active situations, such as fights and beatings. Blood droplets as small as an aerosol spray indicate that the wound was produced by a powerful force, such as a gunshot or an explosion.

Teacher Notes and Key for Lab 2-6, *Cold Blood*

1. This lab requires about 60 minutes. It is best suited for outdoors. If an outdoor area is not available, use indoor slopes such as wheelchair ramps or stairs.

2. A day before the lab, determine how many lab groups you will have. For each lab group, spread a sheet of newspaper on the ground. You can place these papers wherever you wish: on a flat surface, a gentle slope, or a steep slope. Be sure that all papers are placed on the same slope.

3. With a pipette, let a drop of ketchup fall on each newspaper. Measure and record the height from which you dropped the ketchup. Allow the spots of ketchup to partially dry so that you can hand them out in class tomorrow.

Answers to Data Table

Data will vary, depending on the method you used for making your crime scene blood stains.

Answers to Postlab Questions

1. Answers will vary.

2. Answers will vary.

3. Answers will vary, but might suggest that Larson determine whether the crime was committed on flat land, or on a hill. He could use this information to search for the crime scene. The height from which blood was dropped might give some information about the killer's height or about the events occurring just before the victim was killed.

4. a. the droplet's speed at time of impact, b. the direction of the droplet's travel, and c. the size of the droplet.

Name _____ Date _____

Cold Blood
A Lab on Blood-Drop Analysis

Objectives

You will create blood drop patterns from various angles and heights.
You will compare a blood drop from a crime scene with blood drop patterns.

Background Information

Mrs. Kent's dog, Homer, likes to escape from his pen and roam about the neighborhood. Everyone loves Homer, even though he has a bad habit of picking up everything he finds. On one occasion, he brought Mrs. Kent a glove he found in a neighbor's yard. Another time, he dragged home a blanket that he had pulled from a clothesline. Homer's kleptomaniac behavior always embarrasses Mrs. Kent.

This evening, Mrs. Kent arrives home to find that Homer has escaped again. She leaves her groceries and bags in the car and immediately begins calling him. After several minutes, Homer can be seen loping toward her with something in his mouth. When he arrives, the big dog proudly drops his package at Mrs. Kent's feet.

Mrs. Kent is relieved to see that all Homer has brought home tonight is a few sheets of newspaper. They don't even look like new papers because they are dirty and wrinkled. After returning Homer to his pen, Mrs. Kent begins gathering up his mess. She stops when her hand touches something sticky. It looks like blood.

Mrs. Kent stacks the bloody papers on the back porch, then goes into the house to call the police. The police are very concerned about Homer's find, and Detective Larson arrives at her house within a few minutes.

Larson asks Mrs. Kent a lot of questions about what time she got home, what time Homer brought her the papers, and whether or not she had any idea where the papers came from. Larson is excited about Homer's find because early this morning a young woman was found beaten to death in the trunk of her car. Evidence suggested that she had not been killed in the car, and police were looking for any clues that might help catch her killer.

Taking the stained newspaper back to his office, Larson stops by the lab. After giving the lab technician all pertinent data, Larson leaves the papers so that the technician can determine whether or not the blood belongs to the murder victim. Analysis can also reveal the height from which the blood droplets fell, and the angle of the ground on which they fell. These clues might help Larson determine where she was killed.

Materials

Sample of "blood" in 100 ml beaker
Lab apron
Newspapers

Protractor
Plastic knife
Yard or meter stick
Stake
Small board or string
Pen or marker
Sample of "blood droplet" on newspaper from crime scene

Procedure, Part A:
Create a set of bloodstain patterns

1. Go outdoors. Spread four sheets of newspaper across level ground. Put on your lab apron.

2. Dip the plastic knife in the "blood." Holding the knife at a height of 12 inches, walk across one of the newspapers, allowing six or eight drops of "blood" to fall on the paper. Label these as "12-inch blood drops at 90 degrees."

3. Again, dip the knife in the "blood." Holding the knife at a height of 24 inches, walk across another one of the newspapers to create six or eight drops of "blood." Label these as "24-inch drops at 90 degrees."

4. Repeat this process at 36 inches and at 48 inches.

5. Place another four sheets of newspaper on a gentle slope or hillside.

6. Repeat steps 2 through 4 on the newspapers that are spread on the gentle slope.

7. Place another four sheets of newspaper on a steep slope or hillside.

8. Repeat steps 2 through 4 on the newspapers that are spread on the steep slope.

Procedure, Part B:
Comparing a bloodstain from a crime scene with your bloodstain patterns

1. Your teacher will give you a piece of blood-stained newspaper from the crime scene.

2. Analyze the stain by comparing it with the work you did in Part A.

3. Complete the following Data Table.

DATA TABLE
Information of size and shape of blood drop from crime scene.

A. Shape and size of droplet	B. Height from which droplet fell	C. Droplet fell on flat ground, gentle slope, steep slope

© 1998 by The Center for Applied Research in Education

Postlab Questions

1. Was the bloodstain from the crime scene similar to any of the bloodstains you created in steps 1 through 8? If so, which ones?

   _____

   _____

   _____

   _____

2. Based on your work, was the crime committed on a flat area, a gently sloping area, or a steeply sloping area?

   _____

   _____

3. If you were Detective Larson, how would you use the information gathered in lab today to help solve this crime?

   _____

   _____

   _____

   _____

   _____

4. What information can be determined by examining a blood drop?

   _____

   _____

   _____

   _____

LESSON 2-7: FIBERS DON'T FIB!
A LESSON ON FIBER ANALYSIS

Fibers, strands of thread that make up yarn, are all around us. You encounter a variety of fibers each day. Fibers make up thousands of products, including clothing, upholstery, carpet, rope, and building components. As you interact with these products, loose fibers become attached to your body and clothes. When you enter a room, you pick up some of the fibers present in the room. You also drop some of the fibers you are carrying. Therefore, fiber evidence can often provide information about where people have been.

Tracking the Source

For fiber evidence to be useful in a crime scene investigation, scientists must be able to narrow down its origin to one or two sources. Because most clothing, upholstery, and carpet are mass produced, this is sometimes difficult to do. Only under unusual circumstances can a fiber positively identify a person.

Fibers can be divided into two large groups: natural and man-made. The earliest people wore animal skins and furs for clothing. Since the Stone Age, people have been weaving fibers from plants and animals into fabric for clothing. Wool, silk, cotton, flax, and the husks of some dry fruits are examples of natural fibers. From these plant and animal products, people learned to form individual threads that could be woven into large pieces of cloth (see Figure 16). By the time of the Industrial Revolution, weaving was a mechanized process that produced plenty of fabric for a growing population and its needs. However, the fabric industry still depended on nature for its raw materials. Drought, flooding, disease, and cold weather could badly damage the fiber crops and reduce the amount of cloth available.

Made in the Lab

After the Industrial Revolution, scientists began searching for a fiber that could be made in the lab. Such a discovery would provide manufacturers with a constant supply of fibers. About 100 years ago, the first man-made, or synthetic, fiber was created in the lab and named "rayon." Rayon was made by chopping and chemically treating wood pulp and cotton to produce a soft mass of cellulose. This cellulose was then forced through tiny openings in a spinnerette to form threads (see Figure 17).

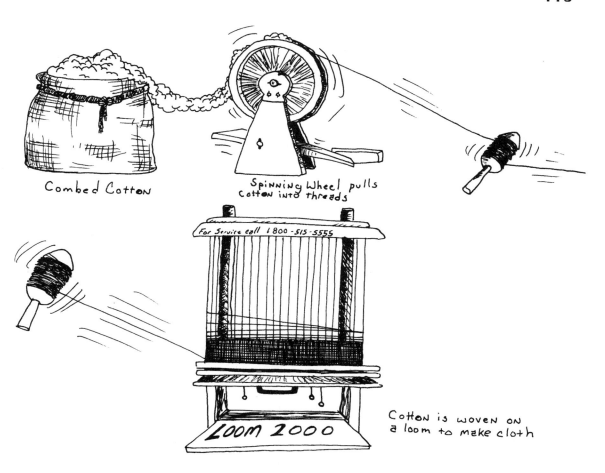

Combed Cotton

Spinning Wheel pulls
cotton into threads

For Service call 1 800-515-5555

LOOM 2000

Cotton is woven on
a loom to make cloth

Figure 16. Thread can be made from cotton. Cotton threads can then be woven to form a fabric.

Until the 1970s, more natural than synthetic fibers were used as raw materials to make products. At the present time, however, about twice as much synthetic fiber than natural fiber is used to make fabric. Many types of synthetic fibers have been invented since the appearance of rayon. Man-made fibers are generally classified into the following two groups, depending on whether or not they originated from cellulose:

a. Fibers derived from cellulose include rayon and acetate.

b. Fibers that are not derived from cellulose include nylon, polyester, acrylic, and spandex.

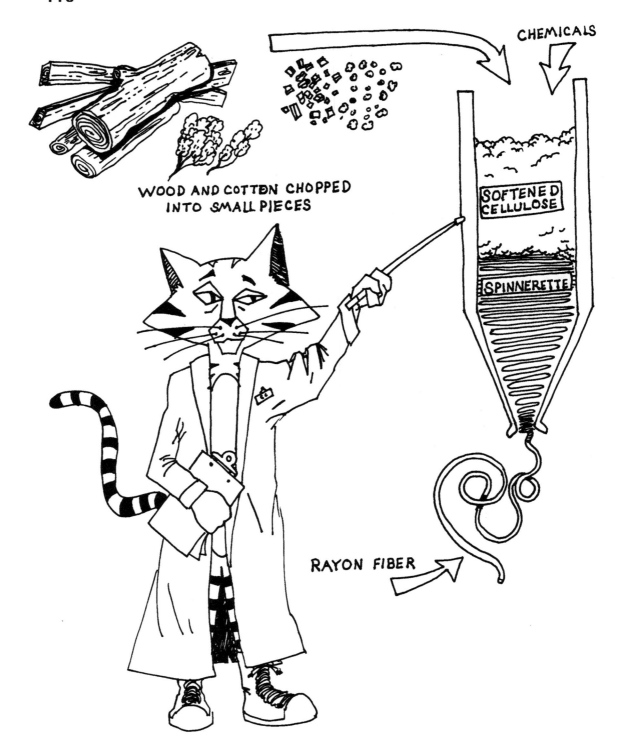

WOOD AND COTTON CHOPPED
INTO SMALL PIECES

CHEMICALS

SOFTENED CELLULOSE

SPINNERETTE

RAYON FIBER

Figure 17. Softened cellulose was forced through a spinnerette to make the first synthetic fiber, rayon.

TEACHER NOTES AND KEY FOR LAB 2-7, *PICKING UP THE PIECES*

1. This lab requires about 80 minutes. It can be divided into two parts: the microscopic examination and the burning tests.

2. Collect samples of fabric made of wool, rayon, polyester, silk, and cotton. If possible, collect all of the samples in red (or the same color). Let polyester be the fiber that is the unknown one found on the victim.

3. Cut out a paper pattern of a victim and place it on the floor or draw the outline of a victim on the floor with chalk. Sprinkle a few polyester fibers on the outline. Place samples of cotton, wool, silk, polyester, and rayon on a table so that students can pull sample fibers from them.

Answers to Data Table

	Approaching flame	*In flame*	*Removed from flame*	*Odor*	*Residue*
Fiber from victim	shrinks away from flame; melts	burns slowly; melts and drips	extinguishes	chemical	hard bead
Wool	curls	burns slowly	extinguishes	hair	hard bead
Rayon	ignites on contact	burns quickly	glows or continues burning	paper	small amount of light, fluffy ash
Silk	curls	burns slowly	extinquishes	hair	black and brittle
Polyester	shrinks away from flame; melts	burns slowly; melts and drips	extinguishes	chemical	hard bead
Cotton	ignites on contact	burns quickly	glows or continues burning	like paper	flully, light gray ash

Answers to Postlab Questions

1. Polyester. The unknown sample and polyester look the same: Three strands of relatively smooth bundles of thread twisted together.

2. Polyester. The unknown sample and polyester both:

    a. melt and fuse when approaching a flame.

    b. burn rapidly in a flame, melt and drip.

    c. self-extinguish when removed from a flame.

    d. produce a strong chemical odor.

    e. leave a hard, tough gray bead as residue.

3. Fibers taken from the crime scene can help an investigator determine who has been on the scene, and where the victims of the crime have been.

4. Casey

Name _____ Date _____

PICKING UP THE PIECES
A Lab on Fiber Analysis

Objective

You will collect fiber evidence, then analyze it to identify its source.

Background Information

On Saturday morning, a woman's body is found in a stairwell of a downtown apartment building. The woman, who was a resident of the building, had been robbed and badly beaten. Crime scene investigators recover seven different types of fibers from the victim's body. Six of these fibers match fabrics in the victim's home. The seventh fiber, a red one, does not match anything belonging to the victim. Neighbors tell the investigating team that the victim hated red, and probably did not own anything that color.

When questioned by police, the woman's next door neighbors reveal that they saw a tall, young man in a red jacket enter the victim's apartment on Saturday night. The night watchman had reports that no one had walked into the building wearing a red jacket on the night of the murder. Therefore, the police assume that the murderer lives in the apartment building.

Police begin questioning all of the tall, young men in the apartment building who own a red coat. They also check the labels in the coats to find out what kind of fibers make up the coat materials. These men are now considered to be suspects.

George, whose red coat is made of wool

Dave, the owner of an expensive silk red coat

Jeff, who has an old red coat made of cotton

Ted, who owns a red rayon coat

Casey, who wears his polyester red coat everyday

Materials

Compound-light microscope
Slide
Cover slip
Forceps
White paper
Candle
Match
Paper pattern of victim
Red fibers
Samples of wool, rayon, silk, polyester, and cotton

Procedure

1. Collect a red fiber from the "victim" by carefully lifting the fiber with a pair of forceps. Do not touch the fiber with your hands. Place the fiber on a piece of white paper, then fold the paper in half twice.

2. Carry the fiber to your lab station. Prepare a wet-mount slide of the fiber by placing it on the slide, adding a drop of water, and covering the fiber and water with a cover slip.

3. Examine the fiber under low, medium, and high magnification of your microscope. Sketch what you see. Note any pits or striations on the fiber.

Low-magnification sketch of crime-scene fiber:
Medium-magnification sketch of crime-scene fiber:
High-magnification sketch of crime-scene fiber:

4. Compare this fiber to known samples of wool, rayon, silk, polyester, and cotton. Sketch each of these samples at the magnification that gives you the best view and record these sketches here.

Known Fiber	Low	Medium	High
Wool			
Rayon			
Silk			
Polyester			
Cotton			

5. Light your candle and compare the burning characteristics of the unknown fiber to the known samples. Record your observations on the Data Table.

a. Holding the fiber in forceps, bring it close to, *but not touching,* a flame. Describe the fiber's behavior as it approaches a flame: does it begin to melt, ignite, curl?

b. Holding the fiber in forceps, touch the fiber to a flame. Does it ignite quickly or slowly? Does it sputter, drip, or melt?

c. Remove the fiber from the flame and describe how it behaves. Does it self extinguish, continue to burn, or continue to glow?

d. Note any odor associated with the fiber in the flame. Does it smell like vinegar or hair?

e. What kind of residue is left after the fiber is removed from the flame? Does the fiber leave a white, fluffy ash, a hard bead, or a melted blob?

DATA TABLE

Behavior of fibers in flame.

	Approaching flame	In flame	Removed from flame	Odor	Residue
Fiber from victim					
Wool					
Rayon					
Silk					
Polyester					
Cotton					

Postlab Questions

1. From your observations of the fibers under the microscope, which type of fiber is most like the unknown fiber taken from the victim? Describe the similarities of these two fibers.

_____

_____

_____

_____

_____

_____

2. From the burning tests, which type of fiber is most similar to the unknown fiber taken from the victim? Describe the characteristics they have in common.

_____

_____

_____

_____

3. Why might an investigator want to identify unknown fibers from a crime scene?

_____

_____

_____

_____

4. Which suspect do you believe committed the crime?

_____

_____

SECTION 3

LIFE SCIENCE LESSONS

LESSON 3-1: DON'T FLUSH THE EVIDENCE
A LESSON ON URINALYSIS

Urine can contain important information that may be useful during a criminal trial. Analysis of urine samples can give results that provide inferences or clues, rather than direct evidence. Once urine tests are conducted, the relevance of the data gathered from these tests must be evaluated.

The Main Ingredient Is Water

The composition of urine varies, depending on diet and physical activity. Urine is about 95% water, but it also contains urea and uric acid. Urea and uric acid are waste products that result from the normal breakdown of substances in the body. Sometimes traces of amino acids can be found in urine, as well as a variety of electrolytes, compounds that ionize in water.

A Liter or Two

The volume of urine produced by one person varies from 0.6 to 2.5 liters per day, depending on factors such as fluid intake, body temperature, environmental temperature, and relative humidity. Urine flows from the kidneys, where it is formed, through ureters to the urinary bladder. It is excreted through the urethra. (See Figure 18.)

Sweet Urine

In cases of diabetes, urine may contain glucose. This is because the cells of diabetics cannot utilize all of the glucose in the blood. Therefore, extra glucose accumulates in the bloodstream and is removed by the urinary system.

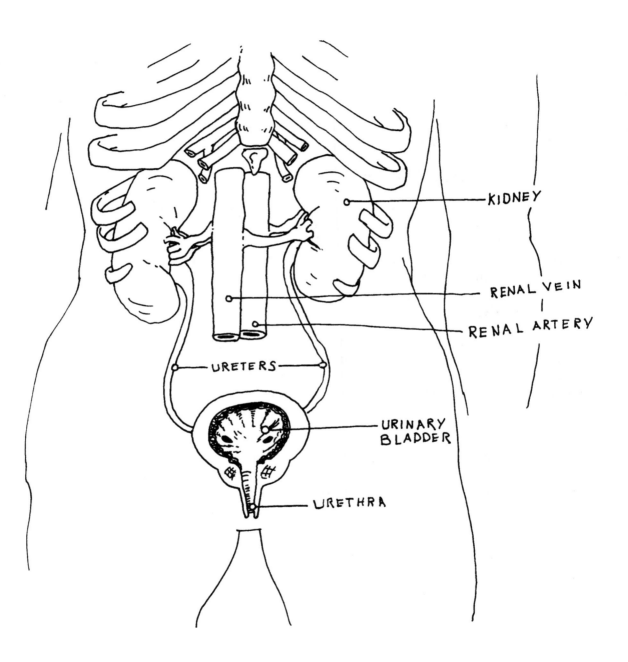

Figure 18. The urinary system.

TEACHER NOTES AND KEY FOR LAB 3-1,
A POOL OF YELLOW EVIDENCE

1. Students need 60 minutes to complete this activity.

2. Purchase three varieties of synthetic urine from a chemical or biological supply house, or make three beakers of synthetic urine, following these recipes:

    ◆ Urine A from the cellar (normal urine):

    > 160 ml water
    > A few drops of yellow food coloring
    > 2 grams NaCl

    ◆ Urine from suspect B: add 40 ml of apple juice (this will give a positive glucose test) to 26 ml of normal urine

    ◆ Urine from suspect C: add a few drops of egg white (this will give a positive test for albumin) to 66 ml of normal urine

Answers to Data Table

Sample	Specific Gravity	pH	Albumen	Glucose
A. Cellar Sample			No	No
B. Suspect 1			No	Yes
C. Suspect 2			Yes	No

Answers to Postlab Questions

1. No. Therefore, the person who stayed in the cellar was not one of the suspects.

2. Sample pH's will average about 7.0.

3. The cells of diabetics are not able to take glucose from the blood and use it for energy.

4. No. However, a urinalysis might eliminate someone who is a suspect.

Name _____ Date _____

A Pool of Yellow Evidence
A Lab on Urinalysis

Objectives

You will perform analytical tests on three urine samples.

You will evaluate the results of these tests as clues in solving a crime.

Background Information

Officers Chan and Langley receive a call from their dispatch officer to proceed to 3230 Lexington Street. They are needed to help investigate a crime scene. A man has been murdered, and police are looking for clues.

On the scene, Chan and Langley find the new widow, Mrs. Davis, sitting with an officer who arrived earlier. This officer is comforting Mrs. Davis and trying to help her understand the crime scene. Things look a little strange, and the police cannot determine what happened.

It appears that Mr. Davis died following a blow to his head. A crowbar is found a few feet from the body. Because the investigative team has already examined the deceased and most of the crime scene, Mr. Davis's body is being removed. Mrs. Davis found him lying on the kitchen floor when she came home from the grocery store. The cellar door was standing open, as if Mr. Davis had started to go down to the storage room. She immediately called 911, then waited with her dead husband until help arrived.

Detective Larson is in charge of the scene, and he meets Chan and Langley when they arrive. "OK, here's what we know. Mr. Davis was hit on the back of the head with a heavy instrument. He was dead when his wife got home. We need to figure out what he was doing, and what happened that caused his death. I've got one team on the main floor, one outside in the yard, and I want you two to check out the cellar."

Putting on rubber gloves so they won't leave their fingerprints, the two officers turn on the cellar light and proceed down the stairs. Each carries a pen and pad for notes, as well as a flashlight. Nothing in the cellar looks suspicious. Everything is tidy and neatly stacked on shelves. An old mattress is standing up against one wall, and jars of home-canned jams are sitting on the shelves. Chan and Langley probe deeper, looking behind and under things.

"Hey, check this out, Chan. Broken glass is pushed behind this box, like someone tried to hide it." Langley is shining his light into a dark corner.

Chan raises her head to answer, then lifts a half gallon jar of yellow liquid from the floor. "Yeah, well look at this stuff. I'm not sure what it is, but it smells pretty bad. I think it's urine."

"Urine, huh? There's a lot of it. Maybe the murderer hid down here in the cellar for a few days. I think this broken glass is the same kind used in those canning jars on the shelf. It looks like the Davises have had a visitor."

Chan and Langley call Detective Larson down and show him what they found. He wants the urine and broken glass sent to the forensic lab immediately. "If we get a suspect, we can use these fingerprints on the glass and this urine to help identify him as someone who was on the scene. Great work!"

Materials

Beaker A containing urine sample from cellar
Beaker B containing one suspect's urine sample
Beaker C containing another suspect's urine sample
Hydrometer
pH paper
Centrifuge
Test tubes
Beakers
Hot plate
Benedict's solution

Procedure

1. Examine the three urine samples. In the Data Table, record their odor, color (yellow, amber, gold, etc.) and clarity (clear, cloudy, etc.).

2. Determine the specific gravity of each urine sample. Specific gravity of a liquid is a comparison of that liquid's mass to the mass of an equal volume of water at the same temperature. The specific gravity of a liquid depends on the components of that liquid. For example, adding salt to water increases its specific gravity.

    a. Remove the hydrometer from its cylinder and empty the water. Fill the hydrometer cylinder three-fourth's full of the urine sample A.

    b. Pour some of this same urine sample in a beaker. With a spinning motion, float the hydrometer in the beaker of urine. (Do not let the hydrometer lean against the sides of the beaker.)

    c. When the hydrometer stops spinning, read the specific gravity at the bottom of the meniscus formed on the hydrometer column. Record this specific gravity on the Data Table.

    d. Pour the sample A urine back into the appropriate beaker.

    e. Repeat step 2 with samples B and C.

3. Dip a small piece of pH test paper into sample A. Compare the color of the paper with the color standards on the pH test paper container. Record pH of the urine on the Data Table. Repeat this procedure with the other two samples of suspects' urine.

4. Test each urine sample for albumin, a protein, by following this procedure:

   a. Centrifuge test tubes of all three urine samples.

   b. Observe the clarity (clear, cloudy, etc.) of supernatant A.

   c. Pour supernatant A into two test tubes (see Figure 19). Label both test tubes as A. Set one aside.

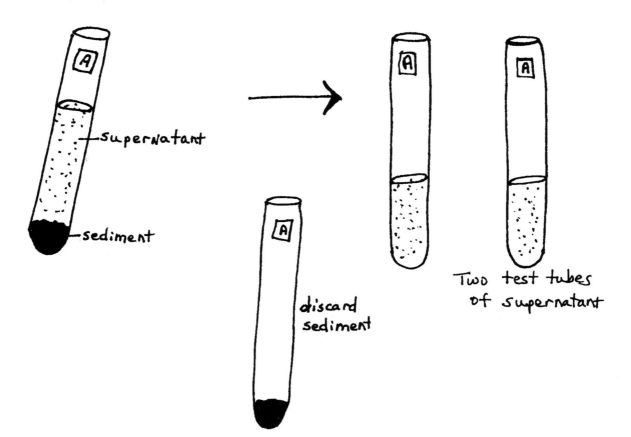

Figure 19. Pour half of the supernatant into another test tube.

   d. Place the other test tube of supernatant A into a hot water bath (see Figure 20) and warm for several minutes.

   e. Compare the clarity of the supernatant after heating to its original clarity. If cloudiness increases when the sample was heated, then albumin is present.

   f. Repeat this procedure with suspect supernatant samples B and C.

5. Test each sample of supernatant for glucose:

   a. Add 10 drops of Benedict's solution to each of the remaining three test tubes of supernatant.

   b. Add 10 drops of Benedict's solution to a test tube of water.

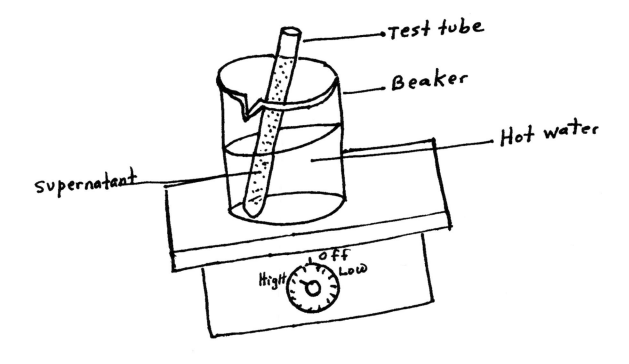

Figure 20. Place a sample of supernatant A into a hot water bath.

c. Place all four test tubes in a hot water bath. After several minutes, observe their color. If the Benedict's solution changes from blue to yellow or gold color, then glucose is present in the urine.

DATA TABLE

Lab results on three urine samples.

Sample	Specific Gravity	pH	Albumen (yes or no)	Glucose (yes or no)
A. Cellar Sample				
B. Suspect 1				
C. Suspect 2				

Postlab Questions

1. Did sample A have the same characteristics of either of the suspect samples? If your answer is yes, what does that mean about the suspect samples? If your answer is no, what does that mean about the suspect samples?

   _____

   _____

   _____

   _____

2. What is the average pH of all three urine samples? (To determine an average, add all of the pH ratings, then divide them by 3.)

   _____

   _____

   _____

   _____

3. Why does glucose accumulate in the urine of diabetics?

   _____

   _____

4. Do you think a urinalysis can be used to definitely link someone to a crime scene? Why or why not?

   _____

   _____

   _____

   _____

LESSON 3-2: THE TEETH WILL TELL
A LESSON ON DENTAL FORENSICS

Dental forensics concerns the application of dentistry to law. In criminal trials, dental forensics can be helpful in two ways: (1) to establish the identity of a homicide victim, and (2) to associate a suspect with a crime using bite-mark analysis.

People can be identified by their teeth because everyone's teeth are different. The average human adult has 32 teeth (see Figure 21). Since almost everyone has been to a dentist, most people have a dental record. This makes teeth a better identifier than fingerprints, since many people have never been fingerprinted.

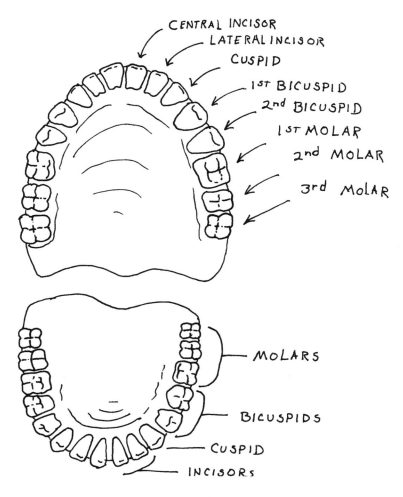

Figure 21. Adults have 32 teeth.

135

Naming Victims

Forensic dentists play an important role in identifying the remains of victims from mass disasters, such as those in the 1995 bombing of the Oklahoma City federal building. Dentists from across the country helped identify 25% of the human remains from that disaster. In a similar case, dentists helped identify many of the victims from the 1994 crash of American Eagle ATR 72 in Indiana. Even though only 9% of the victims' teeth were recovered from the crash, those teeth were used to identify half of the victims.

Bones and Teeth

In another case, a forensic dentist examined eleven of the seventeen victims of Jeffrey Dahmer, a serial killer. This was a particularly gruesome task because Dahmer had disposed of the bodies by placing them in a 50-gallon drum of muriatic acid. The acid dissolved all of the tissues from the bones as well as the roots of single-rooted teeth. What investigators found in and around Dahmer's home were stacks of bones, skulls, and loose teeth. Dentists were able to place the loose teeth back into the skulls from which they came, then match dental records to the teeth.

Don't Bite

Bite mark analysis is a new, exciting method of establishing a connection between a bite mark and a suspect. Bite marks occur primarily in sex-related crimes, child abuse, and assaults. Even though bite marks often include only a limited number of teeth, those teeth that can be identified from the mark often yield significant information.

Teacher Notes and Key for Lab 3-2, *Take a Bite Out of Crime*

1. Students need 20 minutes on Day 1 and 40 minutes on Day 4.

2. After students make their twelve bite marks on Day 1, have them lay these bite marks on a counter to dry. You need to wait two or three days before using these bite mark samples so that the saliva can completely dry. Label six of one student's bite marks as A, six of another's as B, and so on, until you have six sets of six bite marks (A through F).

3. Decide which student will be the criminal. Take this student's other six bite marks and label them as "Crime Scene." Throw away the extra six bite marks from all other students.

4. On Day 4, give each lab group one copy of bite marks A, B, C, D, E, F. Also give each group a copy of the Crime Scene bite mark.

Answers to Postlab Questions

1. Bite marks of suspects that match bite marks found at the crime scene can be used to link a person to a crime scene.

2. Young people have sharper teeth than older people. As people age, they continue to wear the sharp edges off of their teeth.

3. The answer depends on which student's bite marks you choose as the crime scene bite marks.

4. Answers will vary, depending on the bite marks you choose to use in this lab.

© 1998 by The Center for Applied Research in Education

Name _____ Date _____

Take a Bite Out of Crime
A Lab on Dental Forensics

Objective

You will analyze bite marks and use your analyses to solve a mystery.

Background Information

"Dr. Johnson, would you introduce yourself to the jury, please, and explain why you are qualified to testify in this trial?"

"Of course. I am a forensic dentist. That means that I use my knowledge of dentistry to help solve crimes, or help identify unknown persons. I've been involved in dental forensics for the last twenty years, and have testified in many cases."

"Thank you, Dr. Johnson. Let me turn your attention to Exhibit #34—a piece of used chewing gum. Do you recognize this?"

"Yes, I do. This piece of gum was found at the murder scene. When I examined the gum, I found several marks made by teeth. This piece of gum led me to think that we might be able to identify the murderer with these marks. The police were holding two suspects in jail, so I made impressions of their teeth. I also made impressions of the victim's teeth."

"What did you do with those impressions, Doctor?"

"I used those impressions to make test marks in silicone, which has a consistency similar to chewing gum. Then I compared the three sets of silicone test marks to the marks left in the chewing gum."

"Was the gum dropped by the murder victim, Dr. Johnson?"

"No, it was not. The marks in the chewing gum were made by very sharp teeth, one of which was chipped. The victim had rounded, smooth teeth because of his advanced age. You see, young people have sharp teeth. But as a person ages, his or her teeth are continually worn down so that they are no longer sharp."

"Did the chewing gum marks match either of the test marks from the suspects' teeth?"

"Yes, they did. Both of the suspects are young men, and they have relatively sharp teeth. However, that is the only similarity in their teeth. One suspect has an undamaged set of teeth, without any nicks or breaks. However, the other suspect has a broken tooth; his teeth marks perfectly match the marks in the chewing gum. Without a doubt, the used chewing gum at the crime scene belonged to him."

Materials, Day 1

12 pieces of 6 cm × 12 cm white paper
12 pieces of 6 cm × 12 cm carbon paper

Procedure, Day 1

1. Fold twelve pieces of carbon paper in half, carbon side out. Fold twelve pieces of white paper in half. Place the carbon paper inside the white paper. Arrange the other eleven pieces of white and carbon paper the same way.

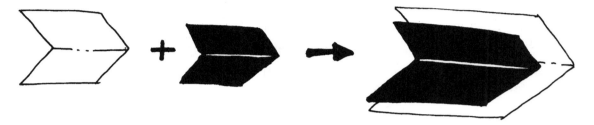

2. Choose one member of your lab group to bite down on all twelve pieces of folded paper. Throw away the carbon, then spread the white paper to dry.

Materials, Day 4

Bite marks from six suspects, labeled A, B, C, D, E, F
Crime scene bite mark

Procedure, Day 4

1. Analyze each bite mark given to you by your teacher. Record information about each mark on the diagrams. For example, if bite mark A has a broken central incisor, draw a broken central incisor on diagram A. When you finish drawing details on diagram A, it should look very similar to bite mark A.

2. Repeat step 1 with bite marks B, C, D, E, F. Record all information on the appropriate diagrams.

3. Analyze the crime scene bite mark, and record information about it in the appropriate diagram.

4. Analyze all of your diagrams to determine which suspect bite mark matches the bite mark from the crime scene.

Postlab Questions

1. How can bite marks be used to help solve crimes?

_____

_____

_____

_____

2. Who has sharper teeth, young people or old people? Why?

_____

_____

_____

_____

3. In the lab today, whose bite mark matched the bite mark from the crime scene?

_____

_____

4. Name the teeth that left impressions in the crime scene bite mark.

_____

_____

Diagrams for Recording Information about Bite Marks

Suspect 1	Suspect 2	Suspect 3
Suspect 4	Suspect 5	Suspect 6
Crime scene		

LESSON 3-3: WHAT A CELL CAN TELL!
A LESSON ON DNA FINGERPRINTING

Since it came into use, DNA fingerprinting has cleared more than 2,000 suspects of false allegations. DNA fingerprinting is based on analyzing an individual's DNA, deoxyribonucleic acid, a molecule which is found in almost every cell of one's body. DNA of all humans is similar, but it varies enough from one person to the next to give each person a unique DNA signature.

The Cell's Plan

The blueprint that nature uses to create every living thing is carried on DNA. This blueprint exists in the nucleus of every cell in that individual, except for red blood cells, which do not contain nuclei. DNA in cells remains recognizable even after the death of that cell. For example, DNA from dinosaurs has been discovered that gives some information about these long-extinct creatures.

DNA Saved the Day

DNA fingerprinting or profiling is a procedure that can determine whether or not a tissue sample came from a particular individual, with 99% accuracy. That is why DNA testing is so useful in clearing individuals of certain accusations. For example, in 1985 a 25-year-old suspect was convicted of raping and murdering a 9-year-old girl in Maryland. The suspect was sentenced to death. Before the sentence was passed, however, it was reversed for technical reasons, and the suspect was tried again. Once more the court found him guilty, but sentenced him to life in prison. In 1993, after spending 9 years in jail, the suspect was released by an order of the governor. The state of Maryland admitted that they had made a mistake in convicting this man, and paid him $300,000 in restitution. This incredible turn of events was due to DNA testing. At the time of his trials, DNA testing was not widely available. However, the sperm taken from the victim had been preserved. Nine years later, investigators were able to take DNA from that sperm and compare it with the suspect's DNA. They found that it was *not* a match.

Making the DNA Fingerprint

To prepare someone's DNA fingerprint, cells are removed from that individual. The DNA is extracted from those cells, then cut into small pieces with restriction enzymes. Because everyone's DNA is different, restriction enzymes cut everyone's DNA into different sizes and numbers of pieces. By analyzing the DNA pieces, an investigator can distinguish one individual from another.

To look at these pieces, the DNA fragments are loaded onto a gel. They are then exposed to an electrical field that causes the fragments to travel through the gel. The rate and distance at which fragments can travel through the gel depends on their size. Eventually, the fragments form invisible bands throughout the gel. These DNA bands are then transferred to a nylon membrane. Radioactive DNA probes are added to the membrane. Then X-ray film is placed over the radioactive probes on the membranes. When the X-ray film is developed, the radioactive probes have exposed it in places where there is DNA. This film makes a DNA print. (See Figure 22.)

DNA testing can also be used in paternity cases. When the parents of a child are not known, the DNA of the parents and child can be compared. Because a child's DNA came from both of his or her parents, comparing the child's DNA with either parent's DNA shows some matches.

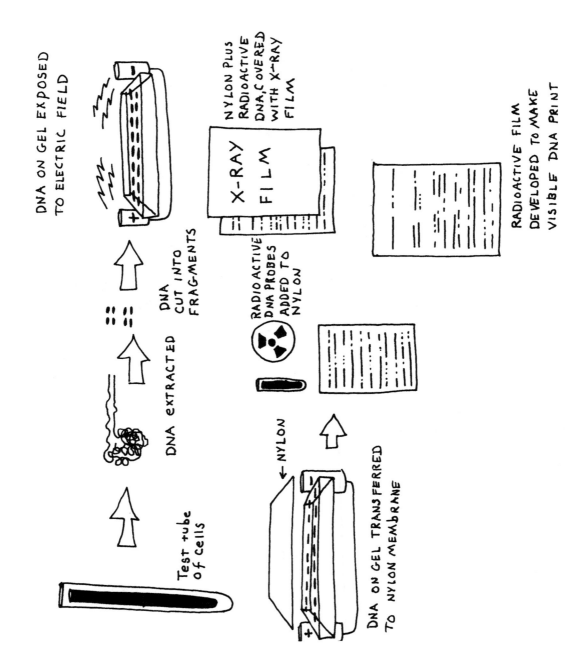

Figure 22. Steps in making a DNA fingerprint.

TEACHER NOTES AND KEY FOR LAB 3-3A, *MISSING PARENTS*

1. Students need 60 minutes to complete this lab.

2. In this lab, students are asked to be creative and draw some fictitious DNA fingerprints, then write a story about them. Therefore, be sure that students understand the information given in Lesson 3-3.

3. Here are possible student drawings. In this case, Couple 2 could have been the parents.

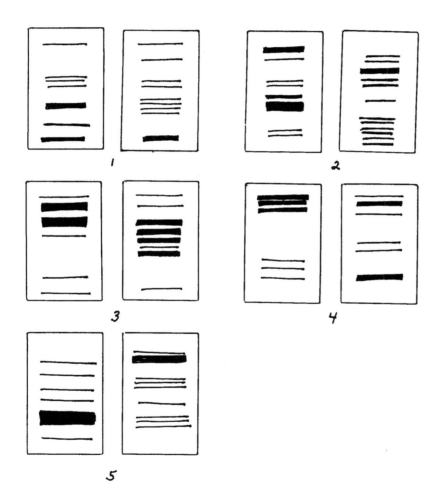

4. Following is an evaluation rubric which you can use to grade this lab.

EVALUATION RUBRIC

Name _____ Date _____

Criteria	Points possible	Points awarded
Five pairs of DNA fingerprints drawn	25	_____
Conclusion to story written	25	_____
Exchanged drawing with classmate and analyzed their work; conclusion written	25	_____
Correctly answered postlab questions	25	_____
Total	100	_____

Answers to Postlab Questions

1. No. A child inherits DNA from his or her mother and father. Therefore, some of the child's DNA will be like the father's, and some will be like the mother's.

2. To prepare someone's DNA fingerprint, cells are removed from that individual. The DNA is extracted from those cells, then cut into small pieces with restriction enzymes. Because everyone's DNA is different, everyone's DNA is cut into different sizes and numbers of pieces. By analyzing the DNA pieces, an investigator can distinguish one individual from another.

3. DNA is in the nucleus of every cell except for red blood cells.

TEACHER NOTES AND KEY FOR LAB 3-3B, INCRIMINATING EVIDENCE

1. Students require 2 to 3 hours to complete this lab. (Teacher preparation time for this lab is 3 to 4 hours.)

2. Buy Edvotek Kit #109 which includes: 6 kinds of DNA that have been cut with restriction enzymes, 1 tube of practice gel loading solution, 4 micro-tipped pipettes, 2 grams of agarose, 1 bottle of electrophoresis buffer, and 2 bottles of methylene blue-staining reagent. Follow the instructions in the kit for preparing the gels. When the kit arrives, store it in the refrigerator. (Call edvotek® at 1-800-388-6835.)

3. If you want students to pour their own gels, they will need one class period to do so. Poured gels can be refrigerated in electrophoresis buffer overnight.

4. Remove DNA samples from the kit and label them appropriately: Suspect 1 is Gloria and Suspect 2 is Suzanne. Suzanne committed the crime. Maintain DNA samples on ice.

Answers to Postlab Questions

1. Suzanne's. When cut with Sma I, her DNA bands matched those at the crime scene.

2. They were the same.

3. They were different.

4. Because cutting their DNA with Eco RI did not show any difference, a second enzyme was used.

5. Stain bands of DNA so they could be seen in the gel.

Name _____ Date _____

Missing Parents
A Lab on DNA Fingerprinting and Paternity

Objectives

You will use fictitious DNA fingerprints to determine paternity.

You will draw some fictitious DNA fingerprints, and write a story about them.

Background Information

Ralph Reynolds is excited today. He may be near the end of a long search. His friends on the police force have been giving him a hard time about his obsession, but he does not care. He plans to find out who his real parents are, no matter what it takes.

Abandoned at a trash dumpster on the day of his birth, Ralph was adopted by Sue and Rodney Reynolds who heard his heart-breaking story on the evening news. Now, 25 years later, Ralph is trying to find out what happened to his birth parents. He is not angry with them, because he loves his adopted family. But he wants to know something about his heritage and his birth family, so he keeps looking.

Since he's been on the police force, Rodney has told his story to several people. Over the years, he has found all of the couples who were living near that dumpster when Rodney was born. The court has ordered these people to donate a small sample of white blood cells for DNA testing. Today, the results of the DNA tests are due. Ralph has his own DNA fingerprint, and he's ready to compare it with the DNA fingerprints of these five couples.

Materials

Ralph Reynold's DNA fingerprint
Scissors

Procedure

1. Examine Ralph's DNA fingerprint.

2. In the following boxes, create DNA fingerprints for the five couples whom Ralph has found. As you draw these fingerprints, decide whether or not you want one of the couples to be Rodney's biological parents. If so, Rodney's DNA fingerprint should show some similarities to both parents' fingerprints.

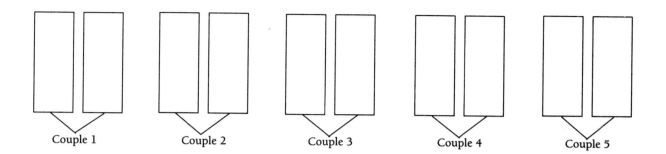

Couple 1   Couple 2   Couple 3   Couple 4   Couple 5

3. On the lines below, write the end of Ralph's story. Base this story on the DNA fingerprints you drew earlier. Keep your story a secret from your classmates. For example, you might:

   a. draw four pairs of DNA fingerprints that are not similar to Ralph's and one pair that is similar to Ralph's. You could then write a conclusion to the background story about Ralph finding his family and the events that followed this discovery.

   b. draw five pairs of DNA fingerprints that do not match Ralph's, and write a conclusion to the background story in which none of these people are his parents.

   c. draw four pairs of DNA fingerprints that are not similar to Ralph's. In the fifth pair of DNA fingerprints, one is similar to Ralph's but the other is not. Write a conclusion to the background story that explains this set of events.

   _____
   _____
   _____
   _____
   _____
   _____
   _____

4. Cut out the DNA fingerprints you drew and exchange them with a classmate. Examine the DNA fingerprints drawn by your classmate. Do you find any DNA fingerprints that matched Ralph's? If so, which one(s)? Record your answers on the lines below.

   _____
   _____
   _____
   _____
   _____
   _____
   _____

5. Cut out your story conclusion and exchange it with the same classmate. Does your answer agree with your classmate's?

Postlab Questions

1. Will a child have the same DNA fingerprint as his or her parents? Explain your answer.

_____

_____

_____

_____

_____

_____

2. How is a DNA fingerprint made?

_____

_____

_____

_____

_____

_____

_____

3. Where is the DNA in your body?

_____

_____

_____

_____

Name _____ Date _____

Incriminating Evidence
A Lab on DNA Gel Electrophoresis

Objectives

You will digest DNA fragments using three different restriction enzymes.

You will run the DNA fragments on a gel electrophoresis apparatus and analyze the results.

Background Information

Johnny Montana, a famous and wealthy movie star, has been murdered. His body was found in his home by the housekeeper. The police have interviewed the housekeeper—and many of Johnny's friends and relatives—to get some clues that might help solve this murder. So far, they have narrowed down the suspects to two women.

Suzanne Montana divorced Johnny 10 years ago. They had been angry with each other ever since the divorce, and Johnny has been jealous of anyone Suzanne met. On more than one occasion, Johnny had been seen at Suzanne's home confronting her about her dates with other men. Everyone knows that Suzanne and Johnny had become enemies.

Gloria Starlight was Johnny's girlfriend. They had been dating for a year, and Johnny had promised to marry her on several occasions. However, something always happened to delay their wedding. Last week Gloria was overheard in a restaurant when she told Johnny that she was tired of playing games with him and it was time to "Get married, or else!"

Blood samples have been taken from Suzanne and from Gloria for DNA fingerprinting. DNA from blood at the crime scene will be compared with DNA from Suzanne and Gloria. To compare their DNA, it must be cut into smaller fragments with restriction enzymes. Two commonly used restriction enzymes are Eco RI and Sma I. These two enzymes cut DNA in two different ways.

Materials

Gloria's DNA cut with Eco RI
Gloria's DNA cut with Sma I
Suzanne's DNA cut with Eco RI
Suzanne's DNA cut with Sma I
Crime scene DNA cut with Eco RI
Crime scene DNA cut with Sma I
Electrophoresis buffer
Micro pipettes
Electrophoresis chamber
Agarose gel

Methylene blue
Aluminum pie plate
Light box
DC power supply
Gloves
Goggles

Procedure

1. Place the agarose gel in its gel bed into the electrophoresis gel chamber.

2. Add enough electrophoresis buffer to the gel chamber to cover the gel.

3. With a clean pipette, place 5 ul. of Gloria's DNA cut with Eco RI into "well 1" in the agarose gel.

4. With a clean pipette, place 5 ul. of Gloria's DNA cut with Sma I into "well 2" in the agarose gel.

5. With a clean pipette, place 5 ul. of Suzanne's DNA cut with Eco RI into "well 3" in the agarose gel.

6. With a clean pipette, place 5 ul. of Suzanne's DNA cut with Sma I into "well 4" in the agarose gel.

7. With a clean pipette, place 5 ul. of DNA from the crime scene cut with Eco RI into "well 5" in the agarose gel.

8. With a clean pipette, place 5 ul. of DNA from the crime scene cut with Sma I into "well 6" in the agarose gel.

9. Place the top on the gel chamber and connect it to the power supply. Plug in the power supply and adjust it to 100 to 150 volts. Run the gel for 30 minutes, or until the samples have almost completely crossed the gel.

10. Turn off the power supply and slide the gel from the gel bed onto an aluminum pie plate.

11. Cover the gel with methylene blue dye. Leave gel in dye for 10 minutes or until blue bands of DNA appear on the gel.

12. Pour the methylene blue into a stock bottle, then rinse the gel in water several times.

13. Place the gel on the light box and compare the crime scene DNA with the other three samples. You are looking for a match.

Postlab Questions

1. According to your results, whose blood was found at the crime scene? How do you know?

_____

_____

_____

_____

2. How does Gloria's DNA that was cut with Eco RI compare with Suzanne's DNA that was cut with Eco RI?

_____

_____

_____

_____

_____

3. How does Gloria's DNA that was cut with Sma I compare with Suzanne's DNA that was cut with Sma I?

_____

_____

_____

_____

_____

4. Why did you use two restriction enzymes in this lab?

_____

_____

_____

_____

_____

5. What was the purpose of the methylene blue stain?

_____

_____

_____

_____

_____

LESSON 3-4: ANIMALS ARE SUPER SMELLERS
A LESSON ON DRUG DOGS

Sight, smell, touch, hearing, and taste; these five senses enable people and other animals to find out about their environments. Humans rely more heavily on their sense of sight than on their sense of smell: they look for clues, read about missing persons, and watch suspicious behavior. In fact, we rarely depend solely on our other senses to give us information. Can you imagine finding a missing person using only your sense of hearing? How about locating an illegal drug using only your sense of smell?

Many animals do rely heavily on senses other than sight. For example, in dogs the sense of smell is at least 200 times as sensitive as it is in people. When a dog walks along a sidewalk, it sniffs the air, the concrete, the soil, and the plants for clues about what has previously passed this way. You never see people behaving in this fashion!

That is why dogs have become so important in police work. Dogs can be trained to detect and lead investigators to many types of smells. Three of these are drugs, explosives, and fire accelerants. Although various breeds of dogs are chosen for this work, Labradors and German Shepherds are two favorites. The breed of dog is not so important as the dog's nature. Trainers look for animals that have the ability to learn and are willing to work.

When a dog is taught to locate a target odor, it can be trained to give one of two types of response: passive response or aggressive response. After detecting an odor, a passive-response dog will sit; when the handler says "Show me," the passive-response dog will point to the odor with its nose. An aggressive-response dog will scratch and bark when it discovers the odor.

Four Types of Searches

Dogs are commonly used by police in four types of searches:

a. *Fire scene searches,* where use of a dog reduces the amount of man hours required by fire and arson investigators. Canines can search large areas in less than half the time it takes a human. This is because dogs are more mobile than people, and have an incredible sense of smell. Some reports suggest that dogs are better at detecting low levels of accelerants than some of the most sophisticated equipment.

b. *Vehicle searches,* where dogs enter vehicles at road blocks or in parking lots to search for drugs, explosives, or fire accelerants.

c. *Crowd searches,* where dogs on leashes mingle among people. Dogs work well in crowds of people because they pose no danger. When a suspect odor is detected on a person, the dog lets its handler know. The canine can then do a direct search of that person.

d. *Area searches,* such as fields or forests, where dogs can quickly cover ground that investigators may never have time or power to check. Evidence found in area searches is often critical in tying a suspect to a crime.

TEACHER NOTES AND KEY FOR LAB 3-4, *CANINE CONSTABLES*

1. Students need 10 minutes on Day 1 and 30 minutes on Day 2.

2. Before the lab, collect six empty film canisters for each lab group. With an ice pick or hot dissecting needle, punch a small hole in the cap of each film canister. For each lab group on Day 1, fill a canister one-quarter full of one fragrance of potpourri powder. This is the "drug" odor that students will try to memorize. Label this canister "A".

3. For each lab group on Day 2, fill the other canisters one-quarter full of other fragrances. Label these as canisters B, D, E, and F. Relabel the canisters used in Day 1 as C. If you wish, mix some of the "drug" fragrances with one of the other fragrances so that one canister contains the drug fragrance and another fragrance. If potpourri powders are not available, use potpourri oils or food flavors dropped on cotton balls.

4. You can use the evaluation rubric on page 156 to grade this lab.

Answers to Postlab Questions

1. Dogs can smell about 200 times better than humans. Therefore, they can help investigators find materials that emit low levels of odors, such as drugs, fire accelerant, or explosives.

2. Answers will vary, but could include:

   a. Fire scene searches, where use of a dog reduces the amount of hours used by fire and arson investigators. Canines can search large areas in less than half the time it takes a human. This is because dogs are more mobile than people, and have an incredible sense of smell. Some reports suggest that dogs can detect quantities of accelerant below the detection limits of sophisticated equipment.

   b. Vehicle searches, where dogs enter vehicles at road blocks or in parking lots to search for drugs, explosives, or fire accelerant.

   c. Crowd searches, where dogs on leashes mingle among people. Dogs work well in crowds of people because they pose no danger. When a suspect odor is detected on a person, the dog lets its handler know. The canine can then do a direct search of that person.

   d. Area searches, such as fields or forests, where dogs can quickly cover ground that investigators may never have time or power to check. Evidence found in area searches is often critical in tying a suspect to a crime.

3. Answers will vary.

EVALUATION RUBRIC

Name _____   Date _____

Criteria	Points possible	Points earned
Data Table completed	33.3	_____
Calculated percentage of students who smelled "drug" on Day 2	33.3	_____
Postlab questions 1 and 2	18.4	_____
Paragraphs written for postlab question 3	15.0	_____
Total	100.0	_____

Name _____ Date _____

Canine Constables
A Lab on Drug Dogs

Objective

You will play the role of a drug dog, and detect a specified odor.

Background Information

Drug-sniffing dogs sweep through Westside High School. Working with police officers who hold the dogs on long leashes, the canines methodically move from one locker to the next.

This unannounced drug search is a surprise to the students and faculty. Conducted during the tenth week of school, it is much earlier than drug sweeps in previous years. At the end of the day, Principal Parson explains to the students and faculty that the county school board has a zero tolerance for drugs in the school, and is willing to work with local police in every way. For that reason, the police are planning to search the school for drugs two or three times a month. The sweeps will be a surprise to everyone, and only the school resource officer will be expecting them. When the K-9 units arrive at school, teachers and students will remain in their classes until the search is over.

On this occasion, the dogs find no drugs. One dog alerts at a locker in the back hall, but a thorough search reveals only schoolbooks. When they finish, the animals and their handlers pack up and visit another high school in the system.

Materials, Day 1

Film canister A (which contains a "drug" odor)

Procedure, Day 1

Smell film canister A several times. In this lab, you will play the role of a drug dog. The "drug" that you are being trained to detect is in canister A. Try to remember its smell for the lab tomorrow.

Materials, Day 2

Film canisters B, C, D, E, F
Calculators *(optional)*

Procedure, Day 2

1. Place film canisters B, C, D, E, F on the lab table. Let everyone in the lab group take turns smelling the contents of the canisters.

2. Have each person in the lab group secretly decide which canister(s) contain the "drug" that you smelled yesterday. When everyone in the group has decided, record each person's response on the Data Table.

3. The teacher will reveal the canister that holds the "drug" odor.

4. Count the number of students in the room. Determine the percentage of students who correctly identified the "drug" odor by using the following formula:

$$\frac{\text{Number of students who identified "drug" odor}}{\text{Total number of students in class}} \times 100 = \underline{\hspace{1cm}}\% \text{ of students who identified "drug" odor}$$

DATA TABLE

Tally of students' names and canister odors identified as the "drug" odor.

Students' names	*Canister(s) (B, C, D, E, F) that contain "drug" odor*

Postlab Questions

1. Why are dogs used at such crime scenes as fires?

_____

_____

_____

_____

2. Name and explain three ways investigators use dogs in police work.

_____

_____

_____

_____

_____

———————————————————

———————————————————

———————————————————

———————————————————

———————————————————

3. Some odors can be remembered longer than others. For some people, a particular odor is always associated with a particular memory. Write a paragraph about the memories that come to mind when you smell: a. hot cookies, b. gasoline, and/or c. rubbing alcohol.

———————————————————

———————————————————

———————————————————

———————————————————

———————————————————

———————————————————

———————————————————

———————————————————

———————————————————

———————————————————

———————————————————

———————————————————

———————————————————

———————————————————

———————————————————

———————————————————

———————————————————

———————————————————

———————————————————

———————————————————

LESSON 3-5: TIME OF DEATH
A Lesson on Forensic Entomology

Entomology is the study of insects and other arthropods. Forensic entomology applies the study of insects to legal issues. It is particularly useful for helping an investigator determine the time of death.

Old Corpse

Sometimes a body is found within a few hours of death. In such cases, time of death can be determined by body temperature and by lividity, which is discoloration of the skin due to pooling of blood. However, if a body is discovered several days, weeks, or months after death, investigators must turn to other methods of determining time of death. One of the most reliable methods is the evaluation of insect life in the corpse.

Insect Food Court

Many types of insects live in and eat dead vertebrates, including humans. These insects play an important role in nature because they help break down and recycle the nutrients that were once tied up in living things. Without such organisms, dead things would not decay and their valuable resources could not be used by other living things.

Babies Grow Up

One of the most common carrion-laying flies is the blowfly. It can find a body within one to three days after death. Once laid, the eggs of flies and other insects go through several stages of development. Its tiny eggs develop into larvae, which appear on day 2 and are about 5 mm long. As the larvae continue to develop through day 5, they can reach a length of 17 mm. Between days 6 and 8, the larvae become restless and move away from the body. The larvae change into cocoon-shaped pupae about 9 mm long. They remain in this form, gradually darkening, until they reach adulthood between days 18 and 24 (see Figure 23).

By knowing the length of each stage of an insect's life, you can use their development as a type of clock to determine how much time has passed since the eggs were laid. This helps investigators determine the time of death.

The period of time between death and deposit of the first egg is somewhat variable. During warm weather, egg-laying occurs faster than it does during cold weather. Rain, wind, and other climatic factors can also effect this time frame.

Bugs Can Tell on You

The types of flies found in the body can be helpful in determining whether or not the body has been moved. Some species of blowflies only lay eggs in corpses that are in full sun. Other species prefer those in the shade, and are found in heavily wooded areas. Species of flies living in urban areas are different from those living in the country. Therefore, if a body is found in the country that contains the larvae of a city-dwelling type of fly, investigators can assume that the body was moved from the city to the country.

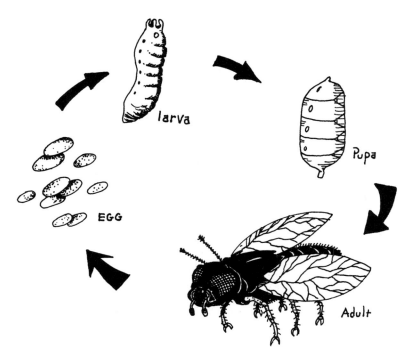

Figure 23. The life cycle of several types of flies includes the egg, larvae, pupa, and adult.

Teacher Notes and Key for Lab 3-5, *Flying Clocks*

1. Students need 30 minutes on the first day, and 20 to 30 minutes on days 2 through 24.

2. If students can collect specimens every day, they can reconstruct a detailed life cycle of these organisms. However, if they only collect every two or three days, they can gather sufficient data to complete the lab.

Answers to Postlab Questions

1. Answers will vary.

2. Answers will vary.

3. Answers will vary, but about 3 to 5 days is a reasonable estimate. Larvae that are 5 millimeters long appear on the second day after egg-laying. These larvae can reach a length of 14 millimeters by day 5.

4. Answers will vary. If more than one species of insect developed in the liver, students may need to draw several life cycles.

5. Over time, the liver lost its dark red color and became brown. Its shape changed from solid to semi-solid, and its odor became increasingly strong and foul.

6. Soft tissue and moisture are associated with body openings; flies find these to be good places to lay eggs.

7. In the orifices as well as in the stab wound where the tissue is soft and moist.

Name _____ Date _____

FLYING CLOCKS
A Lab on Forensic Entomology

Objectives

You will raise carrion flies and collect specimens from each stage in their life cycles.

You will compare the types of carrion flies found in the sunny areas with those found in shady areas.

Background Information

A badly burned body is found in a deserted building that contains stacks of old gasoline and oil cans. The body is not badly decayed. Autopsy reveals that death is due to heart failure. Investigators assume that during the heart attack, the victim accidentally set fire to some papers, which eventually ignited the oil and gasoline.

When found, the body is infested with numerous fly larvae, especially in the ears, eyes, and mouth. The larvae vary in length between 5 and 14 millimeters.

Materials

2 pieces of raw beef liver
2 aluminum pie plates
2 pieces of small-meshed fencing wire, about 1 foot square
Tent stakes
Hammer
Ruler
Dissecting microscope
Hand lens
Tweezers
Collection bottles
Formalin
Sticky fly-paper or fly-trap

Procedure, Day 1

1. Place a piece of raw liver in each aluminum pie plate.

2. Carry the two plates of liver outdoors. Place one in a sunny location and the other in a shady location.

3. Cover each plate of liver with wire. Hammer some tent stakes through the wire to firmly attach the plates of liver to the ground and to prevent animals from eating the liver.

Procedure, Day 2

1. Label two collection jars: one as "Sun" and the other as "Shade." Pour a little formalin in each jar. **CAUTION:** Wear safety goggles when handling formalin.

2. Carry the two jars of formalin, tweezers, and hand lens outside. Observe the meat carefully. There may be more than one type of egg deposited on the meat. Collect a few eggs of each type and place them in the appropriate jar of formalin.

3. Return to the lab and examine the eggs under the microscope. Measure and sketch the eggs, recording all information in the appropriate Data Tables.

Procedure, Days 3 through 24

1. Repeat steps 2 and 3 every day or two, collecting larvae and pupae as they appear.

2. When adult flies begin to appear, hang a sticky fly-trap near the liver to catch them. Remove them from the fly trap and place them in the appropriate jar of formalin. Include measurements and sketches of adults in your Data Table.

Postlab Questions

1. From your experimental results, did you find more insects living in the liver in the sun, or in the liver in the shade?

   _____

2. Were eggs and larvae of the insects living in the sun similar in size and shape to those of insects living in the shade? Describe any differences.

   _____

   _____

   _____

3. Based on your work, how long had the man in the background information been dead? Explain your answer.

   _____

   _____

   _____

4. Based on your work, draw the life cycle of at least one insect from the liver in the sun, and one insect from the liver in the shade. Use another sheet of paper for the life cycle(s).

5. Over the course of the experiment, how did the liver change in shape, color, and smell?

_____

_____

_____

6. When flies find the body of a dead human, they usually lay eggs in the mouth, eyes, and ears first. Why do you think this is so?

_____

_____

_____

7. If a person died due to a stab injury, where would you expect to find a large number of fly eggs? Explain your answer.

_____

_____

_____

_____

_____

_____

DATA TABLE 1

Measurements and sketches of insects (eggs, larvae, and adults) *collected in the sun.*

Days	Measurements of three or more specimens	Sketches of three or more specimens
1		
2		
3		
4		
5		
6		
7		
8		
9		
10		
11		
12		
13		
14		
15		
16		
17		
18		
19		
20		

DATA TABLE 2

Measurements and sketches of insects (eggs, larvae, and adults) *collected in the shade.*

Days	Measurements of three or more specimens	Sketches of three or more specimens
1		
2		
3		
4		
5		
6		
7		
8		
9		
10		
11		
12		
13		
14		
15		
16		
17		
18		
19		
20		

LESSON 3-6: THE THIEF WHO WORE LIPSTICK
A LESSON ON LIP PRINT PATTERNS

One of the first things investigators look for at the scene of a crime is prints. They hope to find fingerprints on items in the house, footprints in the soil outside the house, and even tire prints. One type of print that you do not commonly hear about is the lip print. You have probably seen lip prints at your home. Women who wear lipstick often leave their lip prints on drinking glasses.

Lips, like fingers, have special features that belong only to the individual making the print. Like fingerprints, no two lip prints are exactly the same. Therefore, a lip print can be used to identify an individual.

Many people's lips have parts of at least two patterns. This allows for great variety between the lips of different individuals. When a woman wearing lipstick leaves a print on a surface, an investigator can take that surface to the lab for evaluation or lift the print. When lifting the print, the investigator places talcum powder near the print and spreads it in both directions over the print with a soft brush. After the print is photographed, a piece of clear plastic tape can be placed over the print and then peeled away. The lip print will be transferred to the tape. This print can then be compared with lip prints from suspects.

Lips display five common patterns:

1. short vertical lines

2. long vertical lines

3. rectangular lines that may crisscross

4. lines that form diamond patterns

5. branching lines like those in a plant root

Teacher Notes and Key for Lab 3-6, *Red Lips*

1. This lab requires 20 minutes on Day 1 and 40 minutes on Day 2.

2. All six volunteers must wear lipsticks of the same color. You can use one tube of lipstick, and let students apply it with cotton swabs.

3. The six girls chosen to make the prints on Day 1 will become the suspects on Day 2. After the girls turn in their six prints on Day 1, choose one girl's prints to represent the ones that were taken from the glass at the scene of the crime. This girl's prints represent the one found at the crime scene.

4. On Day 2, have the six girls make one more print each and put their names on the prints. These will be left at the front table for investigative teams to examine.

5. The class should be divided into six groups. Include one of the six suspects in each group. Give each group a lip print from the crime scene.

Answers to Postlab Questions

1. Answers will vary, depending on whose prints the teacher selects on Day 1.

2. Answers will vary, but should indicate specific patterns or combination of patterns.

3. No. She may have been in the bedroom, but there is no proof that she stole the jewelry.

4. Answers will vary, depending on the print characteristics.

Name _____ Date _____

Red Lips
A Lab on Lip Print Patterns

Objective

You will compare lipstick prints to determine who committed the crime.

Background Information

Janice Ayers is the president of the Mayfield Women's Club. Every month the club sponsors a luncheon and invites prospective members. This month the luncheon is held at Janice's home. Six prospects have been invited to attend.

Janice asks the six prospects to wait in the sunroom while the club conducts a five-minute business meeting. The hostess's bedroom is adjacent to the sunroom. While they wait, the women are served lemonade in crystal glasses.

After her guests leave, Janice goes to her bedroom to change clothes. While putting away her jewelry, she discovers that her 2-karat diamond necklace is missing and calls 911. The police arrive within 30 minutes. After a thorough search, the police ask Janice if she brought the crystal drinking glass in the bedroom with her this afternoon. Janice glances at the glass and said, "No, this is one of the glasses used by the prospects. Besides, I don't wear red lipstick."

The investigators speculate that the person who took the diamond necklace must have absent-mindedly left the drink on the dresser. The investigators lift the lip prints from the glass so they can be studied in the lab.

Janice gives police the names of the six prospects who visited her home that day. Investigators visit the women in their homes and have each of them make lip prints on paper for comparison. The police feel that the woman who produces a matching lip print will be the most likely suspect.

Materials

6 tubes of red lipstick (all the same color)
48 pieces of plain white paper, 13 cm × 13 cm
Stereomicroscope
Ruler

Procedure, Day 1:
Creating the evidence with six volunteer students

1. Apply red lipstick to your lips.

2. Fold a piece of white paper in half, and use it to blot your lips. Be careful not to smudge the resulting lipstick print.

3. Repeat steps 2 and 3 five more times on five different pieces of paper so that you have placed your lipstick prints on six pieces of paper.

4. Write your name on a sheet of notebook paper. Carefully fold the six lipstick prints in the notebook paper and give them to your teacher, who will decide which set of prints represents those found at the crime scene.

Materials, Day 2

Lipstick prints from the crime scene
Stereomicroscopes

Procedure, Day 2:
Identification of the criminal

1. The six volunteers who made the lip prints are the six suspects in the diamond theft. Today, these volunteers should:

   ◆ Write their names on the chalkboard.
   ◆ Apply the red lipstick and make one lip print for the class. At the bottom of the print, each volunteer should write her name.
   ◆ Place the lipstick print on a table in the front of the room.

2. Each student, including the suspects, is a member of one of the investigative teams.

3. Examine the crime scene lipstick print under the stereomicroscope.

4. Sketch the crime scene print—noting its special characteristics—on the Crime Report Sheet. Note the line patterns in the lips.

5. Use the stereomicroscope to examine one of the prints made today by the six suspects. Draw this print on the Crime Report Sheet. Note key features about the print and record the name of the suspect.

6. Repeat step 5 until you have drawn and made notes about all six suspects' lip prints.

Postlab Questions

1. Who left the lipstick print on the glass in Janice's bedroom?

   _____

2. Explain what patterns in the lip prints helped you to identify the person who left her glass in the bedroom.

   _____

   _____

   _____

   _____

3. Is this enough evidence to convict the suspect of theft?

   _____

   _____

4. Select someone in your group (who was *not* one of the six suspects) to make a lip print. Describe the patterns you see in that person's lips.

   _____

   _____

   _____

   _____

   _____

CRIME REPORT SHEET

Sketch of lip print taken from scene of crime	*Notes on patterns in lip print*

Sketch of lip print taken from Suspect 1. Her name is _____.	*Notes on patterns in lip print*

Sketch of lip print taken from Suspect 2. Her name is _____.	*Notes on patterns in lip print*

Sketch of lip print taken from Suspect 3. Her name is _____.	*Notes on patterns in lip print*

CRIME REPORT SHEET *(continued)*

Sketch of lip print taken from Suspect 4. Her name is _____.	*Notes on patterns in lip print*

Sketch of lip print taken from Suspect 5. Her name is _____.	*Notes on patterns in lip print*

Sketch of lip print taken from Suspect 6. Her name is _____.	*Notes on patterns in lip print*

LESSON 3-7: ONLY YOUR HAIRDRESSER KNOWS FOR SURE

A LESSON ON HAIR IDENTIFICATION

Hair recovered at a crime scene can be valuable to forensic scientists. Therefore, crime scene technicians collect any hairs that they find and send them to the lab for analysis. Forensic scientists are familiar with hair structure and chemistry.

Follicle Full

Hair grows from follicles, or tiny pockets, in the skin (see Figure 24). The entire surface of a mammal is covered with thousands of these follicles. Located beside each follicle is a small muscle that can make the hair stand upright. A nerve connects the follicle to the brain; that's why it hurts to pull a hair out. A sebaceous gland in the wall of the follicle produces sebum, an oil that is essential for normal hair and skin. The entire length of a hair includes the root, which is embedded in the skin follicle, and extends the length of the shaft to the hair tip.

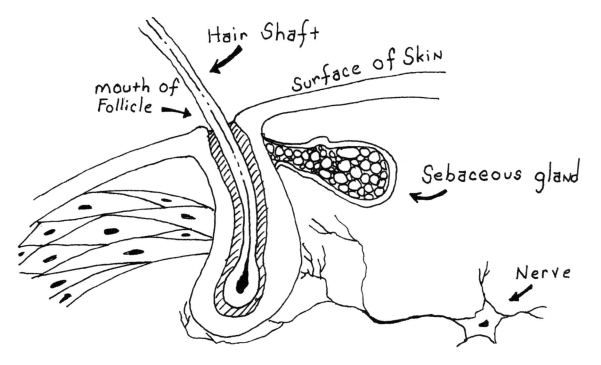

Figure 24. Hair grows from follicles in the skin.

175

Your Scales

A hair is composed of three distinct layers: cuticle, cortex, and medulla (see Figure 25). The cuticle is the hard, outside covering that protects the inner layers of hair. It is made of overlapping scales pointing toward the tip. The scales are cells that have hardened and flattened. There are many different types and arrangements of cuticle scales, varying from loose, open scales to tight, firm scales.

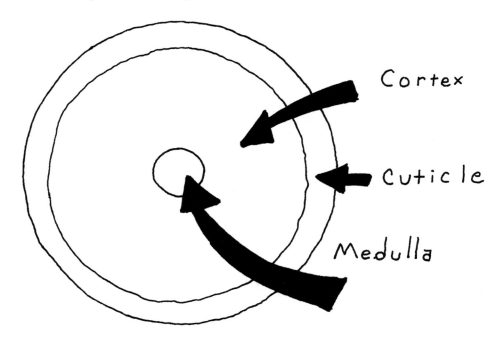

Figure 25. Hair is made of three layers.

Your Hair Color

The cortex is made of cells within the cuticle. Seventy-five to 90 percent of a human hair is composed of cortex. These cells contain the pigments that give hair its color. Forensic scientists sometimes use color, shape, and distribution of pigment granules to tell the difference between hairs of two individuals.

Medullary Patterns

The medulla of a hair is made of cells that run through the center of the cortex like a canal. In humans, this is a very small layer. The medulla may not be a continuous canal: it can be interrupted, fragmented, or absent (see Figure 26). Forensic scientists determine the medullary index of a hair: the diameter of the medulla relative to the diameter of the hair, expressed as a fraction. Humans have a medullary index of less than 1/3. The medullary index of animals is 1/2 or greater.

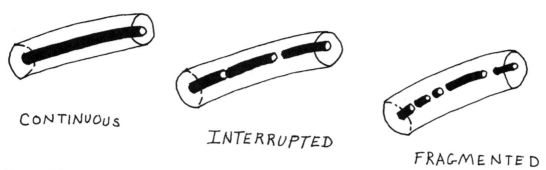

CONTINUOUS

INTERRUPTED

FRAGMENTED

Figure 26. The medulla may be interrupted, continuous, fragmented, or absent.

The shape or pattern of a hair's medulla can help scientists determine its source. In many animals, the medulla makes up most of the cortex. For example, in cats the medulla is arranged like a string of pearls. The medulla of deer hair consists of spherical cells that occupy the entire cortex. Dog hairs have a discontinuous medulla, while hairs of rabbits and mice have large, fragmented medullas (see Figure 27).

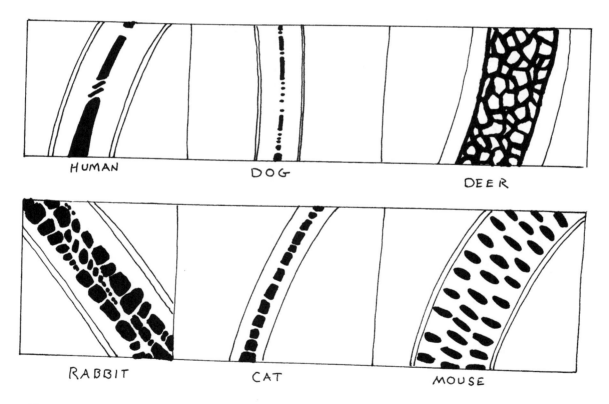

HUMAN   DOG   DEER

RABBIT   CAT   MOUSE

Figure 27. Medullary patterns in human, cat, deer, dog, rabbit, and mice hairs.

Hair Identification

The fact that many humans treat their hair with color or other chemicals can help identify stray strands. Dye can be present in either the cuticle or the cortex of a hair. Bleaching removes the color from hair and gives it a yellow tint. The length of naturally colored "roots" beneath a tinting job is a way of identifying the owner of a hair. Hair grows at the rate of one centimeter per month.

Forensic scientists first determine whether a hair found at a crime scene is a human or animal hair. If it is human, they compare it with the hairs of suspects to see if they can make a match. To do this, scientists use comparison scopes so that hairs can be viewed side by side. If it is animal, they can often identify the animal species.

If the hair under investigation is human, the part of the body from which it originated can usually be determined. Most of the scalp hairs on an individual are about the same diameter. These hairs grow much longer than hairs on the rest of the body. Beard hairs are coarse and have blunt tips from shaving. Pubic hairs are curly and short.

A scientist can sometimes determine the race of a person from samples of his or her hair. Negroid hairs are very curly with densely packed, unevenly distributed granules. Caucasian hairs are often straight or wavy with pigment that is more evenly distributed. In both Negroid and Caucasian hairs, the medulla is discontinuous or absent; however, people of Mongoloid population have a continuous medulla.

Teacher Notes and Key for Lab 3-7A, Hairy Cat Capers

1. Students need 50 minutes to complete this activity.

2. Collect hair samples from five different sources, one of which is a cat. You can use one or more samples of human hair, dog hair, or hair from other animals.

3. For each lab group, prepare 5 envelopes and label them A, B, C, D, E. Place cat hairs in one of the envelopes. As you do this, you are selecting which person in the background information stole Stingray.

4. As an extension, have students write a conclusion to the story presented in the background information.

Answers to Postlab Questions

1. Answers will vary, depending on which envelope contains the cat hairs.

2. Animal hairs have larger medullary indexes.

3. Answers will vary. Cuticle scales are sometimes difficult to see under the compound-light microscope because they appear to be transparent. They might be described as rounded, pointed, or jagged.

4. In this case, crime scene investigators compared hair from the stolen cat with hair samples found in the cars of suspects.

Teacher Notes and Key for Lab 3-7B, Hair Directory

1. Students need 60 minutes to complete this activity.

2. Collect a hair sample from two different dogs of the same species (for example, two different dachshunds) and hair samples from two horses that are the same color. If horses and dogs are not available to you, use any pets that are available. You might contact a local vet for some of these samples.

3. Place samples of several types of hair in ziplock plastic bags, label the bags, and place them in the front of the room for students to pick up.

Answers to Postlab Questions

1. No. It is very difficult to distinguish two animals of the same species that are the same color.

2. Human hair has a thin or discontinuous medulla, scales that are irregular and overlapping, and a rounded bulb.

3. Yes. There is a significant difference in texture, size, and shape of hairs from the head, beard, eyebrow, eyelash, pubis, and armpit.

4. Answers will vary, based on students' personal knowledge. In humans, hair on the head helps the body retain heat; eyebrows divert water, sweat, oils, and other fluids from the eyes; eyelashes keep substances out of the eyes; armpit and pubic hairs retain body odor (a desirable function in early humans). On dogs and most other animals, hair protects and retains warmth.

Name _____ Date _____

Hairy Cat Capers
A Lab on Hair Identification

Objectives

You will compare different types of hair under the microscope.

You will analyze the medulla, cortex, and cuticle of several hair samples.

Background Information

Janis Menendez owns a cat, Stingray, who has starred in several commercials for Flower Fresh Kitty Litter. Before Stingray was a famous cat, she belonged to Penny Jenkins, a full-time college student. Janis agreed to take the cat from Penny several years ago when Penny was too busy to properly care for her. Since Stingray's recent introduction to the world of television, she has earned her owner about $750,000.

On April 2, Ms. Menendez calls San Diego 911 to report that Stingray has been stolen. Menendez states that she was in the family room watching the news while Stingray ate her dinner in the kitchen. Menendez heard a door open, and then a loud screech from the cat. By the time she got to the door, Stingray was gone. All Ms. Menendez saw was a medium-sized car speeding away from her home.

Police who investigate the scene of the crime find no evidence of a forced entry at the kitchen door. Therefore, it is concluded that whoever opened the door and stole Stingray had a door key. Police ask Ms. Menendez for a list of people who drive a medium-sized car and have a key to her house. Her list includes:

a. Joe Menendez, her husband, who loves dogs and is allergic to cats.

b. Bill Branson, a cosmetic salesman whose products are boycotted by Ms. Menendez because they are tested on animals. Susan Branson, his wife, is one of Janis's best friends and knows where the spare key to her house is hidden.

c. Jill Rayburn, a neighbor and cat hater who has poisoned several cats in the neighborhood. Because Jill's kitchen window looks into Janis's back yard, Jill may have seen Janis hide her spare key.

d. Brandy Bledsoe, the maid who often complains that Stingray sheds hair all over the house. Brandy has her own key.

e. Penny Jenkins, Stingray's previous owner and part-time sitter. Penny keeps a key for those occasions when she cat-sits.

Neither Bill, Jill, Brandy, nor Penny own a cat. By evening, the police comb the interiors of their cars to see if they can find any cat hairs.

© 1998 by The Center for Applied Research in Education

Materials

Envelopes containing hair samples taken from the suspects' cars:
A — Joe
B — Bill
C — Jill
D — Brandy
E — Penny
Compound-light microscope
5 slides
5 cover slips
Small beaker of water
Dropper
Small, transparent ruler

Procedure

1. Prepare a wet-mount slide of a piece of hair from Envelope A by:
   a. placing a hair on the slide
   b. adding a drop of water to the hair
   c. covering the hair and water with a cover slip

2. Examine the hair under low, medium, and high power. Draw what you see on high power in the chart.

Sample A	Sample B	Sample C	Sample D	Sample E

3. Determine the medullary ratio of each hair by measuring the diameter of the medulla and the diameter of the hair. Express these two numbers as a fraction in the Data Table.

4. Note the hair length, tip condition, and shape of root in the Data Table.

DATA TABLE

Measurements and characteristics of hair samples A, B, C, D, E.

	Sample A	Sample B	Sample C	Sample D	Sample E
Diameter of medulla					
Diameter of hair					
Medullary ratio					
Hair Length					
Tip condition: Smooth, split, blunt, crushed, frayed					
Condition of root: Absent, rounded, tapered					

© 1998 by The Center for Applied Research in Education

5. Repeat steps 1 through 4 for hair samples in envelopes B, C, D, and E.

Postlab Questions

1. Based on information in your sketches and in the Data Table, which hair sample(s) belong to Stingray?

_____

2. How can you tell human hair from animal hair?

_____

3. When examining the hairs under the microscope, were the cuticle scales clearly visible? Describe their appearance.

_____

_____

4. How can investigators use hair evidence to help solve a crime?

_____

_____

© 1998 by The Center for Applied Research in Education

Name _____ Date _____

Hair Directory
A Lab on Hair Identification of Different Species

Objective

You will collect and describe the hairs of several species of animals.

Background Information

As a trace evidence forensic scientist, you are often asked to identify hairs found at crime scenes. Sometimes you need to know whether or not a hair is human and if not, what type of animal it is from. You also may need to know if two different animals of the same species can be differentiated by their hair. In this lab, you are creating a set of reference hairs to help answer these questions.

Materials

Hair sample 1—from a dachshund
Hair sample 2—from a different dachshund
Hair sample 3—from a brown horse
Hair sample 4—from a different brown horse
Hair samples 5 through 9—from other species of animals
Compound-light microscope
Slides
Cover slips
Small beaker of water
Dropper
Ruler

Procedure

1. Prepare a wet-mount slide of a hair from Sample 1 by:
   a. placing a hair on the slide
   b. adding a drop of water to the hair
   c. covering the hair and water with a cover slip

2. Examine the hair under low, medium, and high power. Draw what you see on high power in the Data Table.

3. Determine the medullary ratio of the hair by measuring the diameter of the medulla and the diameter of the hair. Express these two numbers as a fraction—called the medullary index—in the Data Table.

4. Examine the root of the hair. Sketch that root in the Data Table.

5. Examine the tip of the hair. Sketch that tip in the Data Table.

6. If possible, examine and describe the scales on the hair. Record this description in the Data Table.

7. Repeat steps 1 through 6 for hair samples 2 through 9.

Postlab Questions

1. From the information you gathered, could you tell two different brown rabbits apart by their hair? Why or why not?

   _____

   _____

2. What are some characteristics of a human hair?

   _____

   _____

3. In your set of reference hairs on humans, should you include samples from different parts of the body? Why or why not?

   _____

   _____

4. What are some of the functions of hair in humans? in dogs?

   _____

   _____

   _____

   _____

   _____

   _____

DATA TABLE

Descriptions of hairs from several species of animals.

Hair samples	Species of animal	Sketch of entire hair	Medullary index	Root shape	Tip shape	Scales
1	Dog					
2	Dog					
3	Horse					
4	Horse					
5						
6						
7						
8						
9						

LESSON 3-8: WHAT TYPE ARE YOU?
A LESSON ON INHERITANCE OF BLOOD TYPES

Blood and bloodstains can be important evidence in a criminal investigation. Blood evidence is often used to associate a suspect with a crime or crime scene. From a forensic point of view, blood has several important factors or types. Three of these factors are the ABO system, the MNS system, and the Rh factors.

The ABO Blood System

The ABO system may be most familiar to you because of its importance in blood transfusions. The letters A and B represent two different types of antigens, or molecules, that can be found on the surfaces of red blood cells. A person's red blood cells can be covered with one of the antigens, both of the antigens, or neither of the antigens. Blood types are a reflection of the antigens on the blood cells. There are four ABO blood types (see Table 1).

TABLE 1

ABO blood types are determined by the presence or absence
of antigens on the cells.

Blood type	Name of antigens on blood cells	Blood cells with antigens
A	A	
B	B	
AB	AB	
O	NONE	

The blood of people whose blood cells have type A antigens contains antibodies to type B antigens (anti-B). Antibodies are substances produced by the immune system to help destroy foreign materials. Similarly, the blood of people whose blood cells have type B antigens contains antibodies to type A antigens (anti-A). Blood of type AB does not have any ABO antibodies. Type O blood contains both anti-A and anti-B.

Anti-B antibodies are shaped so that they fit type B antigens. Therefore, anti-B antibodies can cause cells with type B antigens to clump together. Likewise, anti-A antibodies are shaped to fit type A antigens, and can cause type A cells to clump.

Testing for ABO Blood Type

These properties of blood cells help in identifying blood types. If an investigator wants to know what ABO group a blood sample belongs to, he or she can test it with anti-A serum and anti-B serum to see which causes clumping (see Table 2).

TABLE 2

Type A blood clumps with anti-A serum; type B blood clumps with anti-B serum; AB clumps with anti-A or anti-B; and type O does not clump.

Blood Type	Anti-serum	Results
A	A	Clumps
B	B	Clumps
AB	A or B	Clumps
O	A or B	No clumps

You Inherited Your Blood Type

The presence of antigens on cells is genetically determined. Every person can inherit two ABO blood type antigens. If you inherit antigen A from both parents, you will have type A blood.

A Punnett square shows the probable genes of offspring when two individuals mate. The mother's genes, AA, are written across the top of the Punnett square. The father's genes, also AA in this case, are written down the left side of the square. Punnett square 1 shows there is a 100% chance that all of the offspring will have genes AA, and thus type A blood.

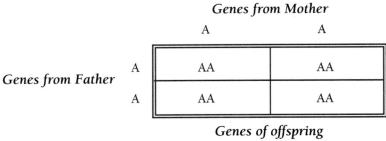

Punnett square 1.

You can also have type A blood if you inherit antigen A from one parent and no antigen (O) from the other parent. The genes of the parents and the possible genes of offspring can be shown in a Punnett square. In Punnett square 2, all of the offspring from a cross of parents with AA and AO blood will have type A blood. Fifty percent will have the genes AA. The other 50% will have the genes AO.

Genes from Mother

	A	A
A	AA	AA
O	AO	AO

Genes of offspring

Punnett square 2.

From this Punnett square, we can see that the mother has type A blood because she has two genes for antigen A. The father has type A blood because he has one gene for type A and one gene for no antigen. Therefore, in the father, the only gene expressed is the one for antigen A.

Each time this couple has a baby, the chances that their offspring will have type A blood is 100%. However, you can see in Punnett square 2 that two of the four squares contain the AA gene combination and the other two contain the AO gene combination. This means there is a 50% chance that each baby will inherit the AA gene combination, and a 50% chance that each will inherit the AO gene combination.

Similarly, if you inherit antigen B from both parents, you will have type B blood. Or, you can have type B blood because one parent donates a gene for antigen B and one parent donates an O gene. Punnett square 3 shows a cross between two parents who both have the genes BB. All of their offspring will inherit the BB genes and have type B blood.

Genes from Mother

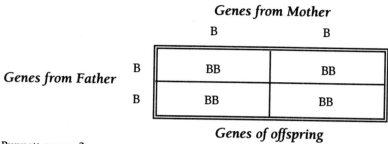

Punnett square 3.

Punnett square 4 illustrates that offspring will still have type B blood, even if one parent has the genes BO.

Genes from Mother

Punnett square 4.

However, offspring will have type AB blood if they inherited antigen A from one parent and antigen B from the other. There are several ways this could happen. If one parent donates genes AA and the other donates genes AB, there is a 50% chance that offspring will have type AB blood. In Punnett square 5, the father has genes AB and the mother has genes AA, so half the offspring will inherit AA and the other half AB.

Genes from Mother

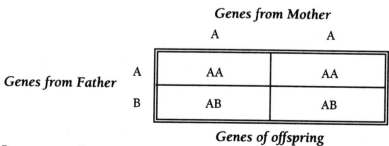

Punnett square 5.

If both parents donate genes AB, there is a 50% chance that offspring will inherit AB blood, a 25% chance that they will inherit AA antigens, and a 25% chance that they will inherit BB. In Punnett square 6, the probable offspring of a cross between an AB mother and an AB father are 25% AA, 25% BB, and 50% AB.

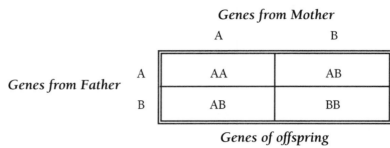

Genes from Mother

Punnett square 6.

Let's look at some combinations of parental genes that could result in a child with type O blood. Since antigens A and B both dominate the type O gene, offspring can only have type O blood if they inherit the O gene from both parents. Therefore, if both parents are type O, there is a 100% chance that an offspring will be type O. If both parents are AO (or BO), there is a 25% chance that an offspring will be type O. Punnett square 7 shows that if both parents carry the genes AO, there is a 25% chance that their offspring will have type O blood. *(OO)*

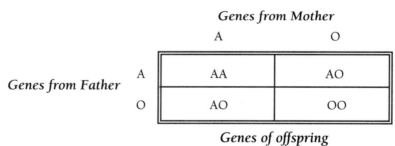

Punnett square 7.

The Rh Blood System

In the Rh blood system, people are classified as either Rh positive or Rh negative. Rh positive people have the Rh antigen on their red blood cells, and Rh negative people do not. If Rh-positive blood is given to a Rh-negative person in a transfusion, the Rh-negative person's blood can make antibodies to the Rh factor. This can cause serious transfusion reactions.

The MNS Blood System

Another, less well-known, blood system is the MNS system. Individuals carry one of these antigens on their blood cells.

Why Type?

Blood typing is useful in forensics because it can show that two samples did *not* have the same origin. Such information is called "exclusion," and is an important aspect of criminology that has freed many criminal suspects. Blood typing is also used to exclude people in paternity cases. The simplest example of such a case would include a woman, her child, and a man who is suspected of being the child's father. Blood typing cannot prove that this man is the father; however, it may be useful if it shows that he is *not* the father.

Blood typing can yield information that narrows down the list of possible suspects. Table 3 shows the percentage of people in the population who have A, B, AB, or O blood. Table 4 indicates the percentage of people in the population who have M, N, and S types. In Table 5, you can see the percentage of people with Rh+ and Rh− blood.

TABLE 3

Percentage of people with A, B, AB, and O types of blood.

Type of blood	Percentage of people with this type
O	45
A	41
B	10
AB	4

TABLE 4

Percentage of people with M, N, and S blood.

Type of blood	Percentage of people with this type
M	30
N	22
S	48

TABLE 5

Percentage of people with Rh+ and Rh– blood.

Type of blood	Percentage of people with this type
Rh+	85
Rh–	15

With this information, you can calculate the possibility that a person would have a particular combination of blood types. For example, to determine the likelihood that a person has blood that is types A, N and Rh-, you would multiply the ratio of all 3 types. To determine the likelihood of an A, N, Rh– combination, look up the percentages each occurs in the population. "A" occurs 41% of the time, or in 41 out of 100 people to give a 2.44 ratio. "N" occurs in 22 out of 100 people, or a 4.55 ratio. "Rh–" occurs in 15 out of 100 people or a 6.67 ratio. Multiply $(2.44) \times (4.55) \times (6.67)$ to get 74. This number can be interpreted to mean than 1 out of every 74 people would have types A, N, Rh– blood.

$$\frac{A}{\frac{100}{41}} \times \frac{N}{\frac{100}{22}} \times \frac{Rh-}{\frac{100}{15}}$$

$$= (2.44) \times (4.55) \times (6.67) = 74$$

This number can be interpreted to mean than 1 out of every 74 people would have types A, N, Rh– blood.

TEACHER NOTES AND KEY FOR LAB 3-8, COULD THE CRIMINAL LIVE IN THIS HOUSE?

1. Students need 40 minutes to complete this activity.
2. Buy simulated type A blood, simulated type B blood, simulated anti-A serum, and simulated anti-B serum from any biological supply house. Let type A blood represent the mother's sample and type B blood represent the father's.

Answers to Data Table

	Anti-A added to sample	Anti-B added to sample	Blood type
Sample 1 (Mrs. Clancey)	yes, clumping occurs	no, clumping does not occur	A
Sample 2 (Mr. Clancey)	no, clumping does not occur	yes, clumping occurs	B

These parents could have a child with O blood if their ABO blood genes were AO and AB.

Answers to Postlab Questions

1. Yes.
2. Yes, if Mrs. Clancey is AO and Mr. Clancey is BO.

Genes from Mother

		A	O
Genes from Father	B	AB	BO
	O	AO	OO

3. Yes, if Rosalyn's genes for ABO blood type are BO.

Genes from Mother

		B	O
Genes from Father	A	AB	AO
	B	BB	BO

4. **AB   N   Rh+**

$$\frac{100}{4} \times \frac{100}{22} \times \frac{100}{85}$$

$$= (25) \times (4.55) \times (1.18) = 134$$

This means than 1 out of every 134 people would have the same blood groups as identified above.

Name _____ Date _____

Could the Criminal Live in This House?
A Lab on Inheritance of Blood Types

Objectives

You will determine the probability of the inheritance of type O blood.

You will determine how many people in the population have the same blood systems as the suspect.

Background Information

Jennifer is jogging along a residential street one evening near midnight. Even though she has been warned that this practice is not safe, Jennifer enjoys being outside at night and chooses to ignore the warning. About 30 minutes after leaving her house, a tall man grabs Jennifer from behind, and tries to force her into a car parked on the street. Jennifer fights desperately with the assailant because she fears for her life. In her struggles, she scratches him several times on the top of the head. Finally, he releases her and runs away. Bravely, she follows after him a short distance and watches him run into the home at 2121 Mocassin Street. However, she never gets a good look at his face. Frightened, Jennifer turns around and runs homes.

When she gets home, Jennifer calls the police and tells them what has happened. Following their instructions, Jennifer meets the police officers at Parkview Hospital Emergency Room where she is examined carefully. The ER doctor finds Jennifer to be in pretty good shape. He takes samples of dried blood from under her fingernails.

Testing of the blood reveals that it is type O. Armed with this information, the police visit the residents of 2121 Mocassin Street. They find that the home is occupied by Sue and Tom Clancey and their two teenage sons, Robert and Blake. Mr. and Mrs. Clancey are appalled at Jennifer's accusations, and refuse to let investigators conduct blood tests on their children. They both state that everyone in the house went to bed about 11 P.M.

As an afterthought, Mrs. Clancey states that she knows her own blood type and her husband's. Because she feels so confident that the police have made an error by coming to their home, she tells them that her blood is type A and her husband's is type B. Paramedics working with the investigating officers take samples of the parents' blood to confirm her claims.

Materials

Simulated blood sample 1 (Mrs. Clancey)
Simulated blood sample 2 (Mr. Clancey)
Anti-A serum
Anti-B serum
4 microscope slides
4 toothpicks
Water
Paper towels

Procedure

To confirm whether or not the parents are telling the truth about their blood types, you will type their blood samples.

1. Place two drops of blood sample 1 on the microscope slide, one drop on each end.

2. Add a drop of Anti-A serum to one of the blood drops. Stir will a toothpick until well mixed. Discard this toothpick.

3. Add a drop of Anti-B serum to the other blood drop. Stir with a different toothpick until well mixed. Discard this toothpick.

4. Observe both drops of blood for evidence of clumping. Record on the Data Table whether or not clumping occurs.

5. Rinse the slide with water, then dry.

6. Repeat steps 1 through 5 with blood sample 2. Record all observations on the Data Table.

7. In the last column of the Data Table, write the blood types of Mr. and Mrs. Clancey.

DATA TABLE
Reactions of samples to Anti-A and Anti-B.

	Anti-A added to sample	Anti-B added to sample	Blood type
Sample 1 (Mrs. Clancey)			
Sample 2 (Mr. Clancey)			

Postlab Questions

1. Did your test results confirm that the parents were telling the truth about their blood types?

_____

2. Draw Punnett squares to demonstrate whether these parents could have a child with type O blood.

Genes from Mother

Genes from Father

3. In the paternity suit, Rosalyn Jones alleges that Jim Smith is the father of her child. Previous tests have shown that the baby has type A blood and Rosalyn has type B blood. A blood test ordered by the court shows that Jim has type AB blood. Is it possible that Jim is the child's father? Draw Punnett squares to explain your conclusions.

Genes from Mother

Genes from Father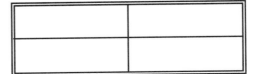

4. Drops of blood found on the shoes of a suspect make police think this man might have been involved in an assault that was committed earlier in the day. During this assault, a young woman was struck on the face with a man's fist, and her blood was spewed in all directions. The suspect denies any knowledge of this assault, and states that he does not know how the blood got on his shoes. The suspect's blood is drawn and is found to be type AB, N, Rh+. How often is this combination of blood systems found in the population?

LESSON 3-9: GIVE IT A TEST

A LESSON ON TESTING FOR THE PRESENCE OF BLOOD

In the field, investigators can perform one of several simple preliminary tests to determine whether or not suspicious brown or red stains are blood. These tests can confirm the presence of one of blood's components, such as hemoglobin. Hemoglobin is the part of blood that carries oxygen and gives its characteristic red color. Hemoglobin is made of two factors: the iron-containing part of hemoglobin called "heme" and the protein part, "globin." One of the preliminary field tests uses hydrogen peroxide to verify the presence of heme. Heme acts as a catalyst that speeds the breakdown of hydrogen peroxide into oxygen gas and water:

$$2H_2O_2 \longrightarrow 2H_2 \quad + \quad O_2$$

Hydrogen peroxide   Water   +   Oxygen gas

Blood Collection

Once a stain is verified as blood, it can be collected and taken to the forensic lab. There are several ways to collect bloodstains at the crime scene:

a. Cut out portions of fabric that are stained with blood.

b. Place fingerprint tape over the stain, rub the nonsticky side of tape with a pencil, then lift the stain. Place the stained tape on a piece of vinyl acetate for easy handling.

c. With a knife or other sharp instrument, scrape the bloodstain into an envelope.

d. Absorb the bloodstain with pieces of cotton thread or small cotton squares that are dampened with distilled water.

In the lab, a stain can be further tested to confirm that it is blood. By mixing it with three different potassium salts and acetic acid, the hemoglobin in the blood will crystallize. The appearance of such crystals is a positive test for blood.

Teacher Notes and Key for Lab 3-9, *Bloodstains on the Ground*

1. Students need 40 minutes to complete this activity.

2. To make bloodstains, drain some blood from a piece of raw beef or chicken liver. The age of the blood does not matter—you can let it dry out if you choose. Make stains on several types of surfaces: tiles, walls, paper, fabric, bricks, etc. If you want to extend the activity, have students test other brown-colored materials: tobacco juice, coffee, brown oil stain, old ketchup, etc. Label each colored material as A, B, C, etc., and tell students to create a Data Table to organize their results.

3. If you don't want students to handle glacial acetic acid, carry out Lab Procedure Step 3 before class, and make mixture available to students.

4. The hemoglobin crystals are very small, rhombic or prismatic in shape, and dark brown in color. Overheating can interfere with crystal formation. The presence of rust can give a false positive test.

5. Be sure students wear safety glasses.

Answers to Postlab Questions

1. Hemoglobin is the part of blood that carries oxygen and gives its characteristic red color. Hemoglobin is made of two factors: "heme" and the protein part, "globin."

2. Heme acts as a catalyst that speeds the breakdown of hydrogen peroxide into oxygen gas and water.

3. a. Cut out portions of fabric that are stained with blood.

   b. Place fingerprint tape over stain, rub the nonsticky side of tape with a pencil, then lift the stain. Place the stained tape on a piece of vinyl acetate for easy handling in the lab.

   c. With a knife or other sharp instrument, scrape the bloodstain into an envelope.

   d. Absorb the bloodstain with pieces of cotton thread or small cotton squares that are dampened with distilled water.

4. Answers will vary, depending on what you used for your brown stain.

5. Answers will vary, but could include cat, dog, horse, rat, hamster, rabbit, fish, lizard, snake, or any other vertebrate.

6. Yes. Criminal investigators usually need to know what kind of blood they are examining.

7. Answers will vary, depending on student results.

Name _____ Date _____

Bloodstains on the Ground
A Lab on Testing for the Presence of Blood

Objective

You will test unknown stains to determine whether or not they are bloodstains.

Background Information

Coming home from school, Samantha approaches her back door slowly. Strange brown stains are all over the concrete walk leading to the house. These are new stains, and Sam does not know their origin. However, they don't seem very important—probably just mud. Removing the house key from her bookbag, Sam opens the back door and walks inside.

"Rambo, here boy" Sam calls. She always looks forward to seeing her sweet little puppy after school. Rambo is usually waiting near the back door, as if he has a watch and knows what time school is out. Today, he is conspicuously absent. Sam feels a little disappointed, and pulls a soft drink from the refrigerator.

"Where could that dog be?" she wonders. Sitting at the kitchen table sipping on her drink, she calls Rambo again.

"Come out, come out, wherever you are, Mr. Rambo. Your favorite person is home." Sam leaves her bookbag and drink in the kitchen and starts walking through the house, looking behind doors and under beds. The dog is nowhere. How can this be? Sam begins to worry a little.

"Maybe he snuck outside this morning when I left for school. There is no telling where he is by now," Sam thinks and she continues her search. The thought of this poor little pampered house dog being outside worries Sam, so she runs back out the door into the back yard.

Continued calling and searching leaves Sam mystified. The brown stains on the walk suddenly take on a new meaning: blood, Rambo's blood. In a panic, she calls the police. Within just a few minutes, a patrol car arrives and two officers join her in the back yard. Sam shows them the brown stains and tells them about Rambo's disappearance.

"Well, you could be right," allows Officer Polasky. "This could be Rambo's blood. But, it could be something else—paint, wood stain, oil, or ketchup. Let me get a little kit out of my car, and we'll check it out."

While Sam waits with Officer Reed, Polasky rummages through his trunk and returns with a plastic box. Inside are several small squeeze bottles. Polasky removes the one labeled "Hydrogen peroxide" and slowly drops a little of its contents on one of the stains. Within less than a second, the peroxide changes to frothy bubbles.

"Yep, it's probably blood," allows Reed. "Let's take some samples down to the lab for another test." Polasky removes a small piece of cotton fabric from the box. After squirting a stain with distilled water, he carefully soaks up the suspected blood with the fabric, then stuffs the fabric in a plastic bag. The officers tell Sam not to worry, and to keep looking for her dog. They promise to call her when the lab results are in.

Materials

Safety goggles (Wear throughout lab.)

Microscope

Slide

Cover slip

Hydrogen peroxide in dropper bottle

Scalpel

White, cotton thread

Distilled water

0.1 g potassium chloride

0.1 g potassium bromide

0.1 g potassium iodide

100 ml of glacial acetic acid

    CAUTION: Strong Acid—In case of contact, flush skin and/or eyes with plenty of water.
    Notify teacher immediately.

200-ml beaker

Stirring rod

Dropper

Tongs

Candle or Bunsen burner

Sample of brown stain

Procedure

1. Examine the suspected bloodstains. To one of the stains, add a few drops of hydrogen per-oxide. Watch the stain for several seconds and record the results of this test in the box. **CAUTION:** Handle all chemicals carefully.

> *Results of hydrogen peroxide test on suspected stain.*

2. Collect some of the suspected bloodstain using the scraping technique, or the white thread technique. Place the collected stain on a glass slide.

3. In the 200-ml beaker, mix 0.1 gram of potassium chloride, 0.1 gram of potassium bromide, 0.1 gram of potassium iodide, and 100 milliliter of glacial acetic acid. Stir gently with the stirring rod. **CAUTION:** Handle all chemicals carefully.

4. Place a drop of the suspected bloodstain on a microscope slide, and add a cover slip.

5. Let one drop of the mixture of potassium salts and acetic acid you just prepared flow under the cover slip and contact the brown stain.

6. Carefully hold the slide with tongs and wave the slide slowly over the candle or Bunsen burner flame. Be careful not to let the slide get very hot. Stop heating the slide when the brown stain begins to bubble.

7. Place the slide on the microscope stage, and examine it under low, medium, and high powers. In the chart below, sketch what you see. The presence of hemoglobin crystals under the cover slip is a positive test for blood.

Sketch under low power	*Sketch under medium power*	*Sketch under high power*

Postlab Questions

1. What is hemoglobin?

_____

_____

_____

2. Why does hydrogen peroxide give a positive test for hemoglobin?

_____

_____

_____

3. What are some ways of collecting suspicious stains at a crime scene?

_____

_____

_____

_____

_____

4. Was your hydrogen peroxide test on the brown stain positive or negative for blood?

_____

5. The test you performed in lab today could not tell you whether a blood sample belonged to a human or to some other animal. Name 10 living things that have red blood.

_____

_____

_____

6. The formation of hemoglobin crystals with potassium salts and acetic acid mixture only tells you that the sample contains a component of hemoglobin. It does not indicate whether the hemoglobin came from an animal or from a human. Is this important to know? Why?

_____

_____

_____

_____

_____

7. Based on your lab results, use the back of this sheet to write a paragraph that explains how the story with Samantha and her dog ends.

SECTION 4

♦

EARTH SCIENCE, ARCHAEOLOGY, AND ANTHROPOLOGY LESSONS

LESSON 4-1: WHERE IS MY MUMMY?
A LESSON ON PRESERVING FLESH

A mummy is a dead person or animal that has been preserved accidentally by nature, or intentionally by people. The process of intentionally preserving a body with chemicals is called embalming. If left unpreserved, a dead body decays quickly. The process of decay is a natural one that is caused by bacteria, protists, fungi, and small animals. When a body is preserved, these organisms cannot live on it, and therefore the body does not rot.

Preparing for a Trip

The ancient Egyptians often mummified their dead because they believed that the dead lived in another world where they needed their bodies. To properly preserve bodies for their trip to the next world, Egyptians spent much effort in perfecting the science of embalming.

Hooks and Jars

Embalming bodies for mummification was a complicated and time-consuming job that could take up to 70 days to complete. In early attempts at embalming, the internal organs were left in the body, which was wrapped in cloth and water-proof resins. Bodies prepared this way often rotted. Later, embalmers learned that the body was less likely to decay if the internal organs were removed and preserved in jars. The brain was removed with a metal hook inserted through a nostril. All of the internal organs, except the heart and kidneys, were removed through a slit in the abdomen. The empty body cavity was refilled with linen cloth or sawdust.

All Dried Up

The body was then put in natron (sodium carbonate) until the tissues were dry. This process caused the tissues to take on a wrinkled, leathery appearance. When preserved, the body was removed from the natron, washed, and rubbed with oils to soften the skin. The dried body was wrapped in many layers of linen cloth and placed in a coffin. The mummy in its coffin was then entombed with objects of daily use that the Egyptians believed the body would need in the next world.

Taking a Peek

Mummies have been discovered in Egypt and other countries during the past 100 years. Unfortunately, many of these treasures were damaged or destroyed by well-meaning people who wanted to determine the identities of the mummified individuals. Today, scientists are able to examine a mummy without even touching it. By taking X-rays and magnetic resonance imaging (MRI) pictures of the body, scientists can get some idea about what is inside the linen bandages. They can often determine age, sex, and cause of death without damaging the mummy in any way.

Teacher Notes and Key for Lab 4-1A, Mummy Manufacture

1. Students need 30 minutes on Day 1, 15 minutes on Days 2 and 7, and 30 minutes on Day 14.

2. Use any kind of meat for this lab except ground meat. Strips of beef, chicken, turkey, or lamb work well. Students need to be able to pick up the meat with a pair of forceps. All meat strips should be about the same size.

3. Caution students to wash their hands after lab.

4. Because of foul odors, you may want to place the meat outdoors during Days 2 through 14. To prevent animals from taking the meat, cover the pieces with wire or screen.

5. Sodium carbonate is also called natrum. It is a salt that was used by the Egyptians to preserve their dead. Sodium nitrate is a preservative used in meats such as bacon and sandwich meat.

Answers to Postlab Questions

1. Bacteria, protists, fungi, and small animals are primary agents of decay.

2. Cold and dry weather conditions, and chemical embalming.

3. Meat samples lost water during the experiment.

4. All of the salted meat lost more water than the unsalted, control sample.

5. Sample E decayed because it was not treated with chemicals to kill bacteria and fungi.

6. Answers will vary. All of these salts will mummify meat, but students may prefer one to the other for personal reasons.

Teacher Notes and Key for Lab 4-1B, Genuine Mummy

1. Students need 40 minutes to complete this lab.

2. Use six shoe boxes with lids to prepare the mystery boxes. Fill each box with a different object, then securely tape the top to the box. Some items you can place in the boxes include: An onion, an orange, a golf ball, a styrofoam ball, a marble, a gumdrop, an eraser, etc. Punch a few small holes in the box so that students can insert their wooden skewers.

3. Have some empty shoe boxes available for students to mass.

4. Here is a sample rubric you can use for grading this lab:

EVALUATION RUBRIC

Name(s)_____   Date _____

Criteria	Points Possible	Points Awarded
Examined all 6 boxes	33.3	_____
Reasonable answers for contents of all 6 boxes in Data Table	33.3	_____
Answered postlab questions correctly	33.4	_____
Total	100	_____

Answers to Postlab Questions

1. Answers will vary.

2. Answers will vary.

3. The box is similar to a mummy because both the box and the mummy are closed to direct viewing. You can get information about both the box and the mummy through methods that give you clues and allow you to make inferences.

4. Answers will vary. Knowing the mass of the contents helps limit one's guesses about those contents.

5. a. D; b. D; c. I; d. D; e. I

Name _____ Date _____

Mummy Manufacture
A Lab on Preserving Flesh

Objective

You will preserve meat in a variety of ways to determine which method gives the best results.

Background Information

"Mrs. Milsap, I'm Detective Lawrence, and this is Dr. Odom from the anthropology department at the university. I brought him along after we got the call about old human remains in your basement. Old remains are Dr. Odom's specialty."

"Thank you for coming. We haven't moved the body since we found it."

"Good, Mrs. Milsap. Tell me how you came across this body."

"We are remodeling the basement, which has a dirt floor. We were trying to smooth the floor so that we can pour concrete. But we found lots of rocks and old bricks that had to be removed. Under a large, flat rock, we found part of a cloth sack with a dried-up-looking person in it. We have no idea how old it is, or how it got there. It looks like the person in the sack is at least 100 years old because the skin is leathery and tough."

Mrs. Milsap leads Detective Lawrence and Dr. Odom down the stairs to the dirt-floored basement, where her husband is standing vigil near the body. Dr. Odom kneels beside the body and examines it closely.

"Well, the person can't have been dead too long. The flesh is still on the bones, and there's hair sticking out of the scalp. Must have died recently, I believe," offers Detective Lawrence.

"Not necessarily, detective," Dr. Odom responds. "This body is very dry, and the basement is cool and dry. Without testing there is no way to know for sure, but this body could be several hundred years old. It is well preserved because it has mummified down here. It may have been here before the house was built."

"What do you mean 'mummified'?" Mr. Milsap asks. "I thought mummies were only found in Egypt."

"Yes, there are a lot of mummies there. But mummification can occur anyplace where conditions are cold or dry. The earliest Egyptians mummified their dead by placing them in the desert in a sitting position. The dry climate removed all moisture from the bodies and preserved them. Later, they soaked the bodies in salts to dry them. This technique is very similar to the one we now use to preserve some meats. In other cases, bodies are mummified by cold weather."

"No matter how old this body is, or how it got here," Detective Lawrence interjects, " I feel certain that a crime was committed. Look at the skull—there's a hole in the back. I think we have a murder case on our hands."

Materials

Goggles

5 meat samples

Wax paper

Ruler

Scale

Labels

Plastic spoons

Forceps

Paper towels

Sodium chloride (NaCl)

Potassium chloride (KCl)

Sodium carbonate (NaCO$_3$)

Sodium nitrate (NaNO$_3$)

Procedure, Day 1

1. Cut 5 small squares of wax paper, about 12 cm × 12 cm. Label these squares as A, B, C, D, E.

2. Place a little piece of meat on each square of wax paper. Find the mass of the meat and paper, and record these masses on the Data Table under Day 1.

3. Cover the meat on paper A with a few spoonfuls of sodium chloride.

4. Cover the meat on paper B with a few spoonfuls of potassium chloride.

5. Cover the meat on paper C with a few spoonfuls of sodium carbonate.

6. Cover the meat on paper D with a few spoonfuls of sodium nitrate.

7. Do not cover the meat on paper E; it will serve as a control.

8. On the Data Table, under Day 1, record the appearance, color, and odor of each piece of meat.

9. Set aside these pieces of meat overnight in a dry place.

10. Wash your hands before leaving the lab.

Procedure, Day 2

1. Observe each meat sample. Record the appearance, color, and odor of each sample on the Data Table under Day 2.

2. With a pair of forceps, pick up meat sample A, hold it over a paper towel, and gently shake any loose sodium chloride from it. Pour any sodium chloride on paper A onto the same paper towel.

3. Place meat sample A on paper A and find their combined masses. Record this mass on the Data Table under Day 2.

4. Replace the sodium chloride you saved on the paper towel onto meat sample A.

5. Repeat steps 1 through 4 with samples B, C, D, and E.

6. Wash your hands before leaving the lab.

Procedure, Day 7

1. Observe the samples and record their appearance, color, and odor on the Data Table under Day 7.

2. With a pair of forceps, pick up meat sample A, hold it over a paper towel, and gently shake the loose sodium chloride from it. Pour any sodium chloride on paper A onto the same paper towel.

3. Place meat sample A on paper A and find their combined masses. Record this mass on the Data Table under Day 7.

4. Replace the sodium chloride you saved on the paper towel onto meat sample A.

5. Repeat steps 1 through 4 with samples B, C, D, and E.

6. Wash your hands before leaving the lab.

Procedure, Day 14

1. Observe the samples and record their appearance, color, and odor on the Data Table under Day 14.

2. With a pair of forceps, pick up meat sample A, hold it over a paper towel, and gently shake the loose sodium chloride from it. Pour any sodium chloride on paper A onto the same paper towel.

3. Place meat sample A on paper A and find their combined masses. Record this mass on the Data Table under Day 14.

4. Discard the meat samples and wax paper.

5. Repeat steps 1 through 4 with samples B, C, D, and E.

6. Wash your hands before leaving the lab.

Postlab Questions

1. What causes a dead organism to decay?

_____

_____

2. What are some ways that decay can be prevented?

_____

_____

_____

3. Why did some of the meat samples lose weight during this experiment?

   _____

   _____

4. Which meat sample lost the most weight during this experiment?

   _____

   _____

5. Sample E was not treated because it was the control in this experiment. Describe what happened to sample E. Why did this happen?

   _____

   _____

   _____

   _____

6. If you were going to mummify a body, which salt would you choose to use: sodium chloride, potassium chloride, sodium carbonate, or sodium nitrate? Why?

   _____

   _____

   _____

   _____

DATA TABLE

Appearance, color, odor, and mass of samples, Days 1 through 14.

Meat Sample	Day 1: mass, color, appearance, odor	Day 2: mass, color, appearance, odor	Day 7: mass, color, appearance, odor	Day 14: mass, color, appearance odor
A				
B				
C				
D				
E				

Name _____ Date _____

Genuine Mummy
A Lab on Mummies and Deductive Reasoning

Objective

You will use deductive reasoning to determine the contents of a closed container.

Background Information

The National Museum received a call from a wealthy man, Mr. Khayat of Cairo, who claims to have the mummy of King Tut's grandson in his home. According to Mr. Khayat, he bought the mummy from an Egyptian family who had been granted the right to keep it by the Department of Egyptian Antiquities. Ordinarily, all ancient artifacts are maintained by the Egyptian government, but this one was an exception. Because the family has suffered difficult financial problems in recent years, they are willing to sell the mummy to a buyer, Mr. Khayat, for one million dollars. Now Mr. Khayat is ready to deal with Dr. Fisher, curator of the museum.

"Thank you for calling, Mr. Khayat, but how do we know that the mummy in your possession is really the grandson of King Tut? What proof do you have? Would you let our forensic anthropologists examine it?"

"Of course not, Fisher! Why, once those scientists unwrap this mummy and poke it with their needles, they will destroy it! I will check with other agencies for a more cooperative buyer."

"Wait, Mr. Khayat. You do not understand my meaning. We can examine the mummy without unwrapping it or damaging it in any way. Of course, we cannot get direct proof that it is the mummy you claim it to be, but we can get plenty of indirect proof. Once we've completed our inspection, we can organize all the clues we've gathered and make some logical deductions. If you have been misled into purchasing a mummy under false pretenses, that is fraud—a serious crime. For your own sake, we should examine this mummy. What do you say?"

Materials

Mystery boxes
Flashlight
Wooden skewer
Empty box
Scales

Procedure

1. Examine the mystery box. Notice that the top is taped closed. Do not remove the tape or open the box.

2. Your assignment is to determine what is in the box without opening it. You may shake the box, turn it, smell it, shine a light on it, weigh it, push wooden skewers into it, tap on it, or examine it in any other way as long as you do not damage it.

3. Determine the mass of a box's contents by following these steps:

   a. Find the mass of the empty box and the mass of the mystery box.

   b. Subtract the mass of the empty box from the mass of the mystery box to determine the mass of the contents.

4. Once you think you know what is in your box, write it down on the Data Table. Then swap boxes with another lab group and repeat steps 1 through 3.

DATA TABLE
Mass and contents of mystery boxes.

Mystery Box	Mass of Contents	Contents of Box
#1		
#2		
#3		
#4		
#5		
#6		

Postlab Questions

1. Which sense—touch, smell, taste, sight, or sound—helped you the most in determining what was in each box? Why?

   _____

   _____

2. How many times did you correctly determine the contents of a box?

   _____

3. How does a closed shoe box represent a mummy?

   _____

   _____

4. Was it helpful to know the mass of the contents of each shoe box? Why or why not?

   _____

   _____

   _____

5. *Deductive reasoning* involves making inferences or drawing conclusions based on available evidence. If you hear the sound of water falling on the roof, and notice that everyone entering the building is wet, you might deduce that it is raining outside. Another type of reasoning, *inductive*, is based on clear evidence. For example, if you walk to the window and see the rain, you have inductively concluded that it is raining.

   Read the following examples and label them as "I" for examples of inductive reasoning or "D" for examples of deductive reasoning:

   _____a. When you walk in the front door, you smell peanut butter and conclude that someone is baking peanut butter cookies.

   _____b. You find your math notebook lying on the floor with teeth marks in it. You feel that your puppy has been chewing on your notebook.

   _____c. You used a thermometer to determine that the temperature of the lake water is 25 °C.

   _____d. Early scientists bombarded atoms with positively charged particles, and found that the nucleus of those atoms repelled the positive charges. This led the scientists to believe that the nucleus of an atom contains one or more positively charged particles.

   _____e. In an experiment, you measured the volume and mass of an unknown liquid, and used this information to calculate the liquid's density to be 1.2 g/ml.

LESSON 4-2: MAKING NO BONES ABOUT IT!
A LESSON ON SKELETAL EVIDENCE

Archaeologists can tell a lot about a dead person's life by looking at all or part of the skeleton. (See Figures 28 A and B.) That is why archaeologists are sometimes asked to assist in solving crimes that occurred in the past. Because of their expertise with skeletal remains, they can often help identify the remains of people who have been dead for a long time. Many times they can determine age, sex, and some information about that individual's lifestyle.

Cartilage Before Bone

Most of the bones in humans develop from masses of cartilage that resemble the bones they will become. The cartilage in bone is gradually replaced with true bone. As long as cartilage is present in a bone, that bone can continue to grow. As people grow, their bones get longer and thicker. That is why an X-ray of a young person's wrist can help his or her physician decide if growth has stopped. If cartilage can be seen at the ends of the bones, there will be further growth; if no cartilage is present, the child has reached full stature.

Growing and Changing

All during life, minerals are deposited and removed from bone. During childhood and adolescence, the deposit of minerals occurs faster than mineral loss; therefore, bones grow. The average female grows until 18 years of age. In males, growth continues to 20 or 21 years. Between the years of 18 and 35, there is a balance of mineral deposit and loss, so bones stay constant in size. After age 35, bone loss exceeds bone gain.

In human adults, the ends of rib bones gradually change shape over the years. The sternal ends are rounded in young adults. These bones become cup-shaped and jagged with increasing age.

Pelvic Girdle Changes

In youth, the pelvic girdle consists of three bones: ilium, ischium, and pubis. These eventually fuse to form the pelvic girdle in adults. The pelvic girdle serves as an area of attachment for bones and muscles of the legs. Females have wider pelvises than males. This additional width is necessary for childbearing and childbirth. In females, the pubic arch is wide, and the bones are lighter and smoother. (See Figure 29.)

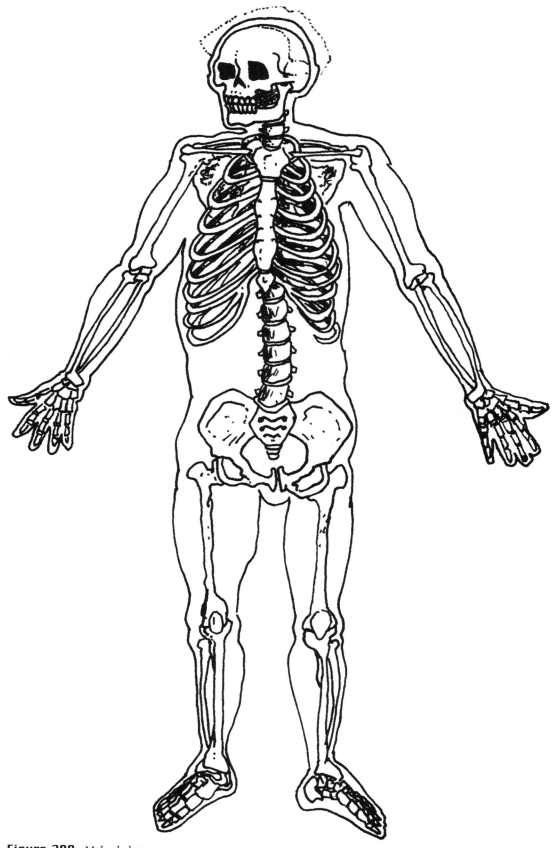

Figure 28A. Male skeleton.

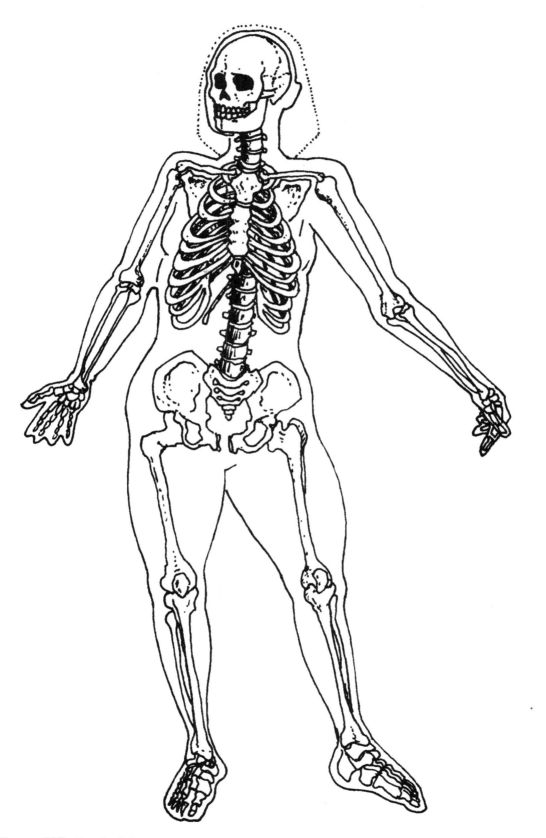

Figure 28B. Female skeleton.

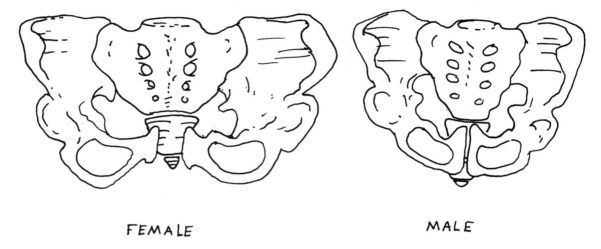

FEMALE   MALE

Figure 29. The pelvic girdle of a female is wider than that of a male. The female pubic arch is wider, and the bones are lighter and smoother.

Male or Female?

When examining a skeleton, forensic archaeologists can determine its sex by examining the pelvic girdle and several other factors:

   a. The female skull is rounder and smaller than the male's. The female forehead is longer vertically, and the jaw is smaller.

   b. The female sacrum is wider and shorter than the male's.

   c. In a female, the coccyx (or tail bone) is more moveable than in a male.

Figure 30 shows a sacrum and a coccyx.

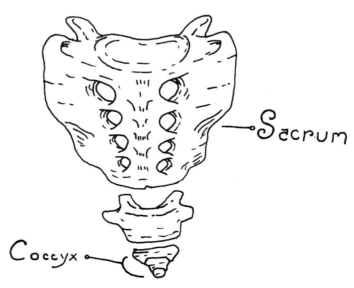

Figure 30. The sacrum and coccyx.

Skulls Grow

The skulls of adolescents and children are quite different from those of adults. At birth, the skull is incompletely developed. The bones of a child's head are not fused together as they are in adults. Instead, they are separated by membranous areas called fontanelles or soft spots. These fontanelles allow some movement between bones, so that the developing skull can be partially compressed and therefore able to change shape slightly. The compressibility of the skull enables an infant to pass through the birth canal. As a child grows, these bones slowly grow together and eventually fuse.

Bones Tell a Story

To determine if a person was right- or left-handed, an archaeologist compares the size of the bones in each arm. Bones in limbs that are used a lot are larger than bones in limbs that receive little use. Similarly, loss of use of a limb can cause the bones in that limb to be small. Injuries and disease are also reflected in bones. Breaks and fractures are generally easy to find. Degenerative bone and joint diseases, such as arthritis and osteoporosis, can be seen in skeletal remains.

TEACHER NOTES AND KEY FOR LAB 4-2A, BONE BONANZA

1. Students need two 60-minute periods to complete this lab.
2. Make a copy of the Skeletal Handout pages for each lab group.
3. If you desire, use the following evaluation rubric to assign grades for students.

EVALUATION RUBRIC		
Name _____		Date _____
Criteria	Points possible	Points earned
Male skeleton assembled correctly	35	_____
Female skeleton assembled correctly	35	_____
Postlab questions correct	30	_____
Total	100.0	_____

Answers to Postlab Questions

1. 38 mm; Grandmother's pelvis is wider than Grandfather's.
2. They were both left-handed.
3. Male and female skeletons have the same number of bones.
4. Both sexes have 12 ribs.
5. Rounded or jagged; as people age, their ribs develop a rounded or jagged shape.
6. Archaeologists can help identify people from their skeletal remains. They can also reveal something about that person's life and health.

TEACHER NOTES AND KEY FOR LAB 4-2B, BITS AND PIECES

1. Students need 60 minutes to complete this lab.
2. Copy the Bone Fragment Handout for each lab group.

Answers to Postlab Questions

1. Yes, Sue Ellen Henderson; the sizes of the bones.
2. Answers will vary, but should include three of the following: the width of the pelvic opening; the width of the pelvic bones; the size and shape of the sacrum; and the angle of the pubis bone.
3. Skulls of females are smaller and rounder than skulls of males.
4. Answers will vary, but should include three of the following: children's bones are smaller than those of adults; children's bones are still growing, and show cartilage; the ribs of children are sharper on the ends than the ribs of adults; and bones of the skulls are not fused.
5. No, because the pelvic bone fragment was part of a wide pelvic girdle. Men have narrow pelvic girdles.

Name _____ Date _____

Bone Bonanza
A Lab on Male and Female Skeletons

Objective

You will separate and reassemble bones of a male skeleton and a female skeleton.

Background Information

Two months ago, police were called to investigate the destruction of a section of Pine City's cemetery. Several gravestones were overturned, graves dug up, and coffins emptied. Based on an eyewitness report, police were able to capture the two perpetrators shortly after the incident.

Following their trial, the judge sentenced these two vandals to a term in prison. He also required them to pay for damage to the cemetery and the costs of reburying each unearthed body.

Two of the victims of this senseless desecration were Sam's grandparents. Sam had never known his grandparents, but he had great respect for them. That is why he had volunteered to be the family member who took care of their cemetery plots. Because his grandparents had never been embalmed, all that remained of their bodies were their skeletons. When the cemetery vandals emptied their coffins, their bones were dumped together and were mixed. Therefore, reburying Grandmother and Grandfather is a difficult task. To sort things out, Sam hires the archaeology professor from the community college. The bill for the archaeologist's services will be sent to the jailed vandals.

Materials

Skeletal Handout
Scissors
Ruler
White paper
Glue
Copies of Figures 28A and 28B from "Making No Bones About It"

Procedure

1. Cut out all of the bones in the Skeletal Handout.

2. Determine which bones belong to Grandmother, and which belong to Grandfather.

3. Reassemble these bones into complete skeletons, using Figures 28A and 28B from "Making No Bones About It" as a guide.

Postlab Questions

1. What is the width of Grandmother's pelvis, measuring from the pelvic brim? How does her pelvis differ from Grandfather's?

   _____

   _____

2. Examine the arm bones of the two skeletons. Was Grandmother right- or left-handed? How about Grandfather?

   _____

   _____

3. Which skeleton has more bones: a male skeleton or a female skeleton?

   _____

4. How many ribs does Grandfather's skeleton have? Grandmother's?

   _____

5. How would you expect the sternal ends of Grandmother's and Grandfather's ribs to look? Why?

   _____

   _____

   _____

6. How can an archaeologist assist a forensic scientist in a criminal investigation?

   _____

   _____

   _____

Skeletal Handout

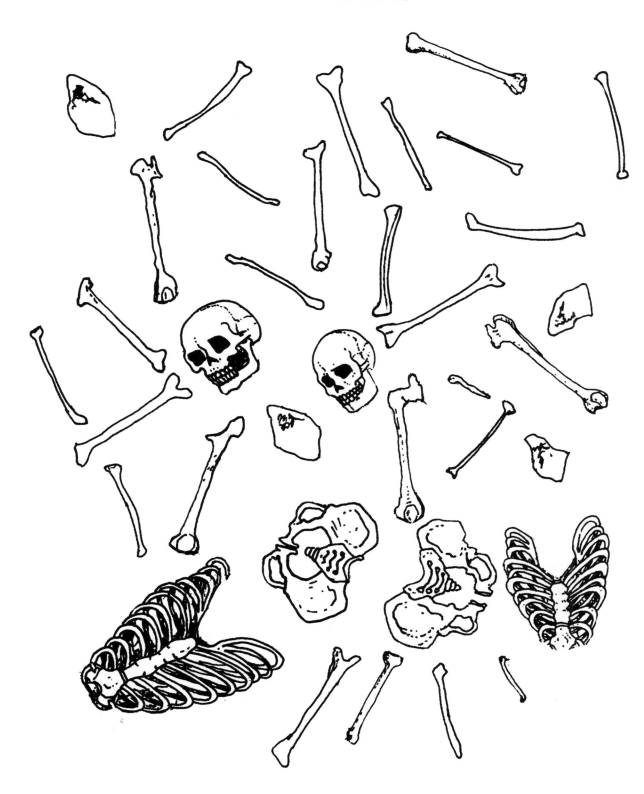

BITS AND PIECES

A Lab on Using Bones to Identify a Missing Person

Objectives

You will identify pieces of bone.

You will use these pieces of bone to identify a missing person.

Background Information

In Springfield, a demolition crew is tearing down the old mill, a fixture in downtown Springfield for about 100 years. The last piece of the building to be removed is the cornerstone. The Springfield City Council plans to display it in Hunter Park. However, the crew has found some bone fragments under the cornerstone, and they have stopped working while investigators and a forensic anthropologist examine the remains.

The bone fragments are taken to the lab, and city records are researched to help determine to whom these might belong. Missing person records from 1899 and 1900 indicate that there were four unsolved cases. Copies of those case records are shown here.

Materials

Bone Fragment Handout

Scissors

Ruler

Procedure

1. Cut out the bone fragments on the Bone Fragment Handout.

2. Compare these fragments to the adult male and female skeletons in Figures 28A and B of "Making No Bones About It."

3. Determine the following and record in the Data Table:

   a. To what bones do these fragments belong?

   b. After examining each fragment, comment on the following:

   ◆ whether the victim was male or female
   ◆ the approximate age of the victim
   ◆ any unusual features of the victim's anatomy

Bone Fragment Handout

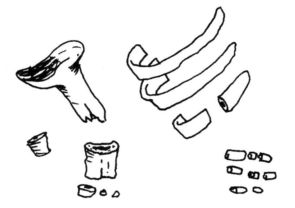

MISSING PERSON REPORT

DATE <u>January 15, 1899</u>   **CASE NUMBER** <u>75342</u>

NAME <u>Dale McPherson</u>   **AGE** <u>62</u>

DESCRIPTION <u>6'1" tall, 210 lbs., brown hair, brown eyes, last seen wearing</u>
<u>overalls and wool coat.</u>

DISTINGUISHING MARKS <u>Injured left leg which caused Mr. McPherson to limp</u>

REPORTED BY <u>Susan McPherson, wife</u>

INFORMATION ON CASE <u>When Mrs. McPherson returned from her sister's home</u>
<u>10 miles away, Mr. McPherson was not at home, and she has not seen him</u>
<u>since. He left no note, which was his custom when he was away from the</u>
<u>house, and had no plans to travel. Mr. McPherson had not been well for the</u>
<u>last five years, and only worked on his farm part time. Because of his illness,</u>
<u>he was in debt to the S & R Bank, a situation that caused him considerable</u>
<u>stress.</u>

INVESTIGATOR <u>Thomas White, Sheriff</u>

MISSING PERSON REPORT

DATE   September 5, 1900   **CASE NUMBER**   81220

NAME   Nell Blankenship   **AGE**   2 years

DESCRIPTION   About 30 lbs., blond hair, blue eyes, toddling, teething. Last seen in a wagon parked outside of Freeman's Feed and Seed on Juniper Street.

DISTINGUISHING MARKS   None

REPORTED BY   Mark and Sarah Blankenship, parents

INFORMATION ON CASE   Mr. and Mrs. Blankenship had ridden into town to get supplies for their livestock. Nell was with them, playing in the back of the wagon with her puppy. When they arrived at the Feed and Seed, they noticed a commotion inside, and jumped out of the wagon to investigate. They found Mr. Freeman wrestling a young man who had tried to steal a bridle. After helping Mr. Freeman subdue the thief, Mrs. Blankenship returned to the wagon to get Nell, but she and the puppy were gone.

INVESTIGATOR   Charlie McAlister, Deputy

MISSING PERSON REPORT

DATE November 7, 1900   **CASE NUMBER** 88342

NAME Sue Ellen Henderson   **AGE** 19

DESCRIPTION 5'4" tall, 112 lbs., last seen wearing a blue dress, feather hat, and boots.

DISTINGUISHING MARKS Large mole on left cheek

REPORTED BY Frank Howell

INFORMATION ON CASE Mr. Howell and Miss Henderson were engaged to be married. On the day of their wedding, November 6, she did not appear at the church. Her parents said that she was gone when they got up that morning. They do not know when she left. Spud Dickerson, clerk at the train station, said that Miss Henderson was sitting at the depot late at night on the evening of November 5.

INVESTIGATOR Charlie McAlister, Deputy

MISSING PERSON REPORT

DATE   November 29, 1900   **CASE NUMBER**   89002

NAME   Florence Rowe   **AGE**   About 70

DESCRIPTION   5′2″ tall, 150 lbs., white hair, loose black dress (last seen by neighbors in August, 1900).

DISTINGUISHING MARKS   Stooped when she walked, persistent cough, fingers disfigured by arthritis

REPORTED BY   Lawrence Adams, neighbor

INFORMATION ON CASE   Mrs. Rowe is a recluse who lives alone and is rarely seen by her neighbors. Mr. Adams believes that she is wealthy, even though she lives in a small home that she maintains by herself. Mr. Adams heard that the late Mr. Rowe left her a lot of money when he died. Mrs. Rowe keeps a small vegetable garden and a few head of cattle. The only reason that Mr. Adams believes that Mrs. Rowe is missing is because he hasn't seen her cows in the pasture for about a week.

INVESTIGATOR   Ralph Prescott, Assistant Deputy

DATA TABLE

Information from examination of bone fragments.

Bone fragment	Bone from which this fragment originated	Comments or details about this bone fragment
A		
B		
C		
D		
E		

Postlab Questions

1. Could these fragments have belonged to any of the missing persons? If so, which one? What evidence supports your answer?

   _____

   _____

   _____

2. How can you distinguish male and female pelvic bones?

   _____

   _____

   _____

3. What distinguishes a male from a female skull?

   _____

   _____

   _____

4. Name three ways you can determine whether a skeleton belongs to an infant or an adult.

   _____

   _____

   _____

5. Could these bone fragments have belonged to a 30-year-old man? Why or why not?

   _____

   _____

   _____

   _____

   _____

   _____

LESSON 4-3: BURIED STORIES
A LESSON ON RECONSTRUCTING PAST EVENTS

Archaeologists are trained to study the remains of human cultures from the distant past. Sometimes this training is helpful in reconstructing events from the recent past. For example, an archaeologist played an important role in determining what, if any, war crimes had been committed in the Ukraine in 1942. Rumors of mass murders had circulated among survivors for 50 years. In 1992, charges were brought to the Australian War Crimes Prosecutors against the Germans, stating that thousands of innocent men, women, and children had been shot and buried in an area of the Ukraine called Serniki.

The Attorney General's Department wanted to prosecute the Germans for this alleged crime. They knew that there were two types of defense the Germans might use: (1) that the wrong person or persons had been charged with the crime, and (2) that the alleged events were imagined. An archaeologist was recruited to make sure that the second type of defense would not be a possibility.

Finding an Unmarked, 50-Year-Old Grave

First, the archaeologist and his team explored the Serniki area on foot, looking for evidence of a large, 50-year-old grave. They were fortunate in finding an area where there was a definite change in the color and texture of the soil. They were able to determine the boundaries of the mass grave by the fill dirt that had been placed in it. The grave was 40 meters long and 5 meters wide.

Soldiers helped the archaeologist by removing the top two meters of soil with bulldozers. Then, the scientist and soldiers worked together to take dirt out of the grave, one shovelful at a time. When bodies were exposed, they finished removing dirt from around them with paintbrushes. The task of uncovering the bodies required five weeks of backbreaking work.

Assembling the Puzzle

By the time they had explored the entire grave, 550 skulls had been found and the archaeologist had a good idea about what had happened in this field 50 years earlier. He found that most of the skeletons were those of women and children. There were a few old men there also. He believes that all of the adults had been herded into the grave and told to lie down, face down, with their hands clasped behind their heads. Most of the victims had been shot, and their skulls showed entry and exit bullet wounds. A few had been clubbed to death.

Dirt had been thrown over the bodies of these adults, then the children were marched into the mass grave and killed in a similar manner. Jewelry and clothing had been stripped from all of the prisoners by the German soldiers as they entered the grave. Articles of clothing that the soldiers did not want were thrown on top of the dead children.

Testimony

At the trial, this archaeologist testified that the rumors of mass murder were true and accurate. He explained that fir trees had been planted on top of the grave filling. The fir trees grew in neat, parallel rows and were clearly part of a plantation. By removing some of the trees and counting their growth rings, the archaeologist could show that the killings occurred during a period of time that agreed with the rumors. Because of his expert work, the court found that a war crime had been committed.

TEACHER NOTES AND KEY FOR LAB 4-3A, *AS IT WAS IN THE PAST*

1. Students need 60 to 90 minutes to complete this lab. It is not necessary for students to completely reconstruct the book.

2. Any short novel will work in this lab. Choose a book that the students have not read. Be sure the book is written on their reading level. You may want to destroy some pieces of the book so that students have to make a few assumptions. To add realism to the lab, damage some of the pages with water, fire, chemicals, food, etc.

3. Cooperation among members of a lab group—and among different lab groups—is vital for this lab. Instead of appointing leaders among the students, let them appoint their own. Learning how to work on a project with such a large group is an important skill.

4. When students have completed their work on the lab, tell them the plot so that they'll know how well they did.

Answers to Postlab Questions

1. Answers will vary. Students were probably unable to completely reconstruct the book.

2. Answers will vary. Students may feel they made intelligent and logical guesses about the book. Others may feel frustrated with the entire project.

3. Reconstructing a book represents reconstructing an event from the past. Like artifacts, some of the pages were missing and others were damaged. Information that was available was not necessarily in the correct order.

4. Answers may vary. Archaeologists probably do not find all of the evidence of past life, unless the place and event they are researching is recent history.

5. As time passes, more and more evidence is lost or destroyed, making the work of archaeologists even more difficult.

TEACHER NOTES AND KEY FOR LAB 4-3B, *TELL THE TALE*

1. Students need 60 minutes to complete the lab.

2. If you do not have five or six old purses that you can prepare for this lab, use plastic bags. The appearance of a real "purse" is not essential to the lab, but it does lend credibility to the entire scenario.

3. In each purse, include these items: copies of airline tickets, credit card, private eye's card, Jiffy store receipt, Family Clothes Care receipt (all given here). Also include some personal items such as photos, play money, pens, pencils, gum, etc. Do not include lipstick, compact, comb, or hair spray.

July 22   12:48 P.M.

SKY VIEW RESTAURANT

Atlanta Airport

Coffee	1.25
Coffee	1.25
Cheesecake	2.00
Ice cream	3.00
SUBTOTAL	$7.50
tax	.45
TOTAL	$7.95

Aero Airlines:	Flight 781	
Departing:	Montreal at 7:50 A.M.	July 22
Arriving:	Atlanta at 11:12 A.M.	July 22

Please arrive at the airport 1 hour before departure time.

Aero Airlines:	Flight 80	
Departing:	Atlanta at 6:00 P.M.	July 22
Arriving:	Montreal at 10:33 P.M.	July 22

Please arrive at the airport 1 hour before departure time.

KEEP THIS STUB TO RECLAIM YOU CAR

Park and Drive   July 22, 6:57 A.M.

Rates:

6 hours	$ 8.00
12 hours	$16.00
24 hours	$30.00

Park and Drive is not responsible for valuables left in your car.

BANK CANADA CREDIT CARD

1121   2222   2234   5757

exp 9/99

Lucinda Piller

PRIVATE EYES

You have questions—we find answers.

Blade Cunningham   342 Peachtree Street   404-998-7777

BANK OF MONTREAL   Deposit Slip

Date of Deposit: <u>July 19</u>   Amount of Deposit: <u>$500,000</u>

Account Number   45699000393 993 9 234

Electronic Key   307

Dear Lucinda,

Meet me at Jake's cafe, 8 pm, July 23. Very Important.

Chris

NAME Lucinda Piller   DATE 7/20

Doctor Christophe Mansuay
Doctors' Pavilion
Montreal

AZT 50 mg
Take two 3X daily

SIGNATURE C. Mansuay, M.D.

Family Clothes Center
Montreal

July 19

Suit	7.50
Blouse	3.00
Subtotal	10.50
Tax	.70
TOTAL	$ 11.20

July 17	8:02 P.M.

Jiffy Stop

Antacid	2.20
Aspirin	1.12
Bandaids	2.53
Newspaper	50
Orange juice	79
tax	.50
Total	$7.64

4. If you desire, use the following evaluation rubric to assign grades to students.

EVALUATION RUBRIC

Name(s) _____ Date _____

Criteria	Points Possible	Points Earned
Completed Data Table with plausible answers:		
• Name of purse owner—Lucinda Piller	10	——
• Last date owner had purse—July 22	10	——
• Events of week before purse was lost— — Visited cleaners, doctor, convenience store; received letter; inquired about PI	25	——
Conclusion to story in background information is plausible and consistent with evidence	30	——
Answers to postlab questions	25	——
Total	100	

Answers to Postlab Questions

1. Answers will vary. The absence of certain personal care items does not necessarily mean anything about the owner of the purse.

2. Answers will vary. Much of the evidence in the purse suggests that she lives in Montreal.

3. Because Lucinda buys aspirin, antacid, and carries a prescription for AZT, students might conclude that she does not feel well, or that she has AIDS.

4. Her note from Chris suggests that he (she) might be a friend. There is not enough evidence to conclude that Blade Cunningham is a friend.

5. Answers will vary. Students might suggest that Lucinda was somehow responsible for removing the arm from a man who attacked her. Alternately, the arm could belong to Chris, or to someone else.

Name _____ Date _____

As It Was in the Past
A Lab on Reconstructing Past Events

Objectives

You will examine bits of evidence to reconstruct a story.

You will compare this activity to the work of archaeologists.

Background Information

Stories have been circulating that several grisly murders occurred in an old community in eastern Europe that is now in ruins. According to legend, the entire town participated in the murders. Many think that the town's mayor and his family controlled the population's behavior by bribing them with opium. After becoming addicted, the residents obeyed the mayor with few questions. When he ordered them to bring strong, young men to his home and kill them, they did so. The legend goes on to tell how the mayor believed that if he drank the blood of these men, he would be strong and young again. The mayor's purported obsession for blood may have been a true story.

You and your classmates are members of a national team of archaeologists. You have spent the summer sifting through the remains of this community. It is now winter, and all of the collected artifacts have been brought indoors for close examination. The job of this team is to examine these artifacts and determine whether or not the legends are true. That is, by examining remaining evidence of life in this community, your group will learn about life in this village 500 years ago.

Materials

Pieces of a novel

Glue or tape

White paper

Procedure

1. Pieces of a short novel are scattered all around your classroom. These pieces of novel represent a series of events that occurred in the past. Some of the pieces may be missing, and others might be damaged. Many are out of order.

2. Work with your lab group and the entire class (the national team) to reassemble as much of the book as possible. Paste or tape the book back together on white paper.

3. Read the reassembled pages and record names and descriptions of characters in the Data Table. Summarize the book's plot, based on the evidence you found.

DATA TABLE

Summary of information found by reconstructing the book.

Names of Characters	Description of Characters

Summary of Plot

Postlab Questions

1. Were you able to completely reconstruct the book's plot? How do you know?

   _____

   _____

   _____

2. When you found that there were missing pieces of the book, were you able to make intelligent guesses about what information may have been in these pieces?

   _____

   _____

   _____

3. How does this book represent events that have occurred in the past?

   _____

   _____

   _____

4. When archaeologists reconstruct a site where people have lived in the past, do you think they find all of the evidence? Why or why not?

   _____

   _____

   _____

   _____

5. As time passes, evidence decays or is washed away from its original location. How does this affect the work of archaeologists?

   _____

   _____

   _____

   _____

Name _____ Date _____

TELL THE TALE

A Lab on Using Inferences to Reconstruct Past Events

Objectives

You will examine bits of evidence from a purse found at a crime scene.

You will compare this activity to the work of archaeologists.

Background Information

The Crime Scene Investigation team has just finished examining, sampling, and photographing a bloody stairwell. What appears to be a man's arm is lying at the top of the stairs. The arm is quite large and hairy, and has a wedding ring on the ring finger.

Near the arm is a woman's purse, splattered with blood. Leading away from the arm are two sets of bloody footprints, one pair larger than the other. You and your investigative team are assigned the job of learning as much as possible about the owner of the purse from its contents.

Materials

Purse and its contents

Procedure

1. Empty the purse onto your lab table. Examine its contents.

2. Determine who owns the purse, the last date the owner had this purse, and recent events that occurred in the life of its owner. Record this information on the Data Table.

3. From the information you gathered, write the end of the story that was presented in the background information.

DATA TABLE

Summary of information found in purse.

Name of owner	Last date owner had purse

Events in last week	

Conclusion of story presented in background information	

Postlab Questions

1. This purse did not contain lipstick, a compact, or comb. Does this suggest anything about its owner?

_____

_____

_____

_____

2. Where do you think the owner of the purse lives? Why?

_____

_____

_____

_____

3. If possible, describe Lucinda's health.

_____

_____

_____

_____

4. Does the purse indicate that Lucinda has friends? If so, describe them.

_____

_____

_____

_____

5. Based on the evidence at the crime scene, what do you think is the relationship between the arm and the purse?

_____

_____

_____

_____

LESSON 4-4: DIGGING UP THE PAST
A LESSON ON INVESTIGATING AN ARCHAEOLOGICAL SITE

An archaeologist is a detective who tries to find clues about life in the past. Like detectives, archaeologists collect information and use it to answer questions or solve mysteries. However, detectives primarily work with the living, and archaeologists work with the dead.

Archaeologists don't just go outside and start digging. They try to maximize their chances of success by looking for a site. When walking over an area, these scientists look for clues of past human life such as a piece of pottery or an arrowhead. Before digging the site, they draw a detailed map of the area. Oftentimes, they try to find out what's under the soil with radar and other remote-sensing devices.

Oldest on the Bottom

When archaeologists start digging, they do so slowly and carefully. They painstakingly remove only one thin layer of earth at a time. By doing so, they can be certain that they have not destroyed the order in which these layers of earth were deposited. Generally, the youngest layers are on the top; the oldest, on the bottom.

By digging slowly, archaeologists do not disturb the arrangement of artifacts in the ground. Artifacts include dishes, garbage, and clothing. They give clues about how people in the past lived, and what happened to them at the time of their death.

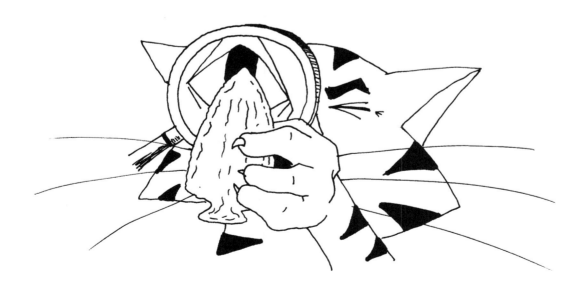

TEACHER NOTES AND KEY FOR LAB 4-4, *DIG A LITTLE DEEPER*

1. Students need 60 minutes to complete this lab.

2. Cut out the drawings of people and objects in Figure 31. Notice that these people are wearing clothes that were stylish in the 1950s. They do not have on shoes. The female has a puncture wound in the chest; the male, a gunshot wound to the head.

3. Pour several inches of potting soil or sand in a small box. Place the two people, the gun, and knife in the sand. Add more soil on top of these objects, then place the man's shoes and one of the woman's heels in the sand. Add a little more soil, then place the other high-heel shoe on top of it. (See Figure 32.)

Answers to Postlab Questions

1. A pair of a man's shoes and one high-heeled shoe.

2. An adult male, an adult female, a gun, and a knife.

3. Answers will vary. Students might speculate that these two people killed each other. However, that explanation does not account for the fact that they were buried, and their shoes buried on top of them. Most likely, these people were murdered by someone else who wanted it to look like they killed each other.

4. Archaeologists are trained to examine sites of previous life in a way that preserves the clues.

5. So they will not disturb the position in which artifacts are lying.

6. Shoes, clothing, gun, knife.

Figure 31. People and objects to be buried in box of soil.

Figure 32. Place the people, the knife, and the gun in a deeper layer of soil than the shoes.

© 1998 by The Center for Applied Research in Education

Name _____ Date _____

DIG A LITTLE DEEPER
A Lab on Investigating an Archaeological Site

Objectives

You will record the dig of an archaeological site.

You will analyze your findings and try to reconstruct the events that created the site.

Background Information

"Thanks for coming out here, Professor Moshier. I know that you have archaeology classes to teach and I appreciate your willingness to drop everything and help me. It looks like we're going to need your kind of advice today," Sheriff Taylor said.

"Glad to be here, Sheriff. Tell me why you need my help."

"Steve Jackson is that kid over there holding a bike. His mom called me when he got home from school today. It seems that he took a short cut through the woods, and found part of an old-fashioned high-heel shoe. It had apparently been buried, but was partially uncovered by last night's rain. One doesn't find many high heels out here, and we're worried that some foul play may be involved. Since this is going to be a digging job, I decided to call you."

"Great. Let me get my equipment and mark off the site. I don't want anyone to walk across it until it's completely mapped. Then we'll start moving dirt, a little at a time, and see what we find. This may take several days. Is that OK with you?"

"Sure. I'd rather have it done right. I have a feeling that if a crime was committed out here, it wasn't done lately. That is a very old high-heeled shoe."

Materials

Box of soil
String
Tape
Graph paper
Ruler
Scissors
Level
Spoons
Small bucket
Empty box

Procedure

1. Draw a detailed map of the dirt in the box. Note any unusual mounds, plants, or artifacts.

2. Measure the length of the sides of the box with the ruler. Mark the sides in 10-centimeter intervals (see Figure 33).

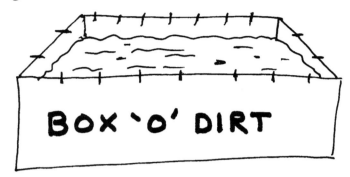

Figure 33. Mark the sides of the box in 10-centimeter intervals.

3. Run a piece of string across the box from one mark to another so that it touches the dirt. Make sure the string is level. Continue in this way until you have formed a grid of strings across the box (see Figure 34).

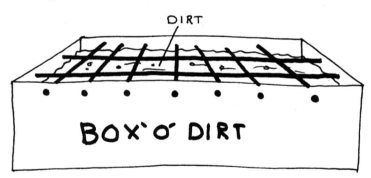

Figure 34. Run strings from one side of the box to the other, so that you form a grid of string across the box. The string should be touching the dirt.

4. As you work, record everything you find in the box on a piece of graph paper. Gently push aside strings. Begin digging by removing a single layer of dirt from the box. Remove just a spoonful at a time, and transfer it to the empty box. Remove dirt to the same depth across the entire box.

5. Continue removing one thin layer of dirt at a time until you find something. When you do, measure the depth from the string grid to the object you found. Record that depth on the Data Table. Sketch the object you found in the appropriate place on your piece of graph paper.

DATA TABLE

Objects found during excavation of site.

Objects/People found	Depth (in centimeters)

Postlab Questions

1. What objects did you find when you first began digging?

   _____

   _____

2. What objects did you find deeper in the site?

   _____

   _____

3. Based on the information you gained by digging in this site, write a paragraph about how you think these two people died. Does your answer take into account the location of the victims' shoes?

   _____

   _____

   _____

   _____

4. Why might an archaeologist be better qualified to solve an old crime than a detective?

   _____

   _____

   _____

   _____

5. When archaeologists work at a site, why do they remove only one layer of dirt at a time?

   _____

   _____

   _____

   _____

6. What artifacts were found at this site?

   _____

   _____

LESSON 4-5: THE DIRT ON CRIME
A LESSON ON EVIDENCE FROM THE SOIL

What exactly is soil? The definition of soil can vary depending on whom you ask. Farmers consider soil to be the top 6 to 12 inches of the earth's crust where plants grow. Geologists—scientists who study the earth's surface—define soil as the organic (carbon-containing) and mineral matter composing the earth. Engineers look at soil as material that can be removed from an excavation site.

Soil and Crime

Forensic geologists consider soil as earth material that has been collected accidentally or on purpose and is related to the matter being investigated. When a forensic geologist is investigating a crime, all natural and artificial objects that are on or near the surface of the earth are considered part of the soil. This includes rock, minerals, vegetation, glass, paint, asphalt, etc. The presence of these objects in that area helps to make that area of soil unique from other areas.

Soils Vary

Many scientists agree that no two places on Earth have precisely the same soil. Soil from one area will be identifiably different from the soil collected in another location. The properties of soil also vary depending on the depth from which the sample is taken.

In most forensic cases, only about one cup of the top layer of the soil needs to be collected. The sample should be allowed to air dry to prevent further decomposition of the material in the soil. Once dry, it is transferred to the crime lab to compare with the soil sample that was found on the suspect or on his or her belongings.

In the Lab

Once in the crime lab, scientists use color as their main identification technique. Before observing the color, all samples are further dried at 100° Celsius for one hour because wet soil will appear as a different color from dry soil. The presence of certain minerals in the soil can give it a characteristic color. For example, the presence of copper minerals appear green while black minerals point to the presence of manganese and iron. Odor and texture of soils are also examined during the initial observation.

Teacher Notes and Key for Lab 4-5, Dirty Characteristics

1. Students need 50 minutes to complete this activity.

2. Collect soil from four different locations. Dry each sample of soil in the oven for one hour at 100° C.

3. Decide which of the four samples you want to call "CS" (the sample from the crime scene) and place part of that sample in a plastic bag. Label that bag as "CS." Label the other four plastic bags as 1, 2, 3, and 4. Fill them with the four soil samples.

Answers to Postlab Questions

1. Answers will vary, depending on which soil sample you chose as the "CS" sample.

2. Capillary action tests the soil's ability to absorb water.

3. Answers will vary, but may include: the top portion of the earth's crust used for plant growth; the earth's surface; the organic and mineral part of the earth; that part of the earth removed from an excavation site; or an earth material collected accidentally or on purpose for an investigation.

4. Soil is dried because wet soil has a different color and a greater mass than dry soil.

© 1998 by The Center for Applied Research in Education

Name _____ Date _____

Dirty Characteristics
A Lab on Evidence from the Soil

Objective

You will compare soil samples taken from the crime scene with soil samples taken from the shoes of suspects.

Background Information

Billy Barron's house was robbed last night. Police discover a window latch broken on the south side of Billy's home. They believe this is how the intruder entered the house. Heavy rainfall the night of the burglary washed away any trace of footprints.

The crime scene investigators guess the burglar might have a lot of dirt and debris caked on his shoes. Therefore, they take a soil sample outside Billy's house and send it to the crime lab for safe keeping.

Early this morning, police bring in four suspects for questioning. None of these individuals can account for their whereabouts last night. Police scrape the bottoms of their shoes and send these scrapings to the crime lab for comparison with the soil in Billy's yard.

Your job is to determine if the soil from any of the suspect's shoes matches the soil outside of Billy's window. Each soil sample has been dried for 1 hour at 100° Celcius.

Materials

5 petri dishes
5 soil samples (in labeled plastic bags)
5 beakers
5 funnels
Graduated cylinder

Stereomicroscope
Measuring scales for mass
Weighing paper
Gauze
pH hydronium paper
Rubber band

Procedure

1. Label five petri dishes with the following letters:

   CS—Crime scene (this is the known sample from Billy's house)
   S1—Soil from Suspect 1
   S2—Soil from Suspect 2
   S3—Soil from Suspect 3
   S4—Soil from Suspect 4

2. Sprinkle enough of each soil sample in the appropriate petri dishes to cover the bottom of the dishes.

3. In Data Table 1, record the following about each soil sample:

   a. Colors

   b. Odors

   c. Textures (grainy, smooth, hard, etc.)

   d. Presence of plant or animal debris

   e. Presence of any inorganic (nonliving) material

4. Repeat step 3 using the stereomicroscope. Record your findings on Data Table 2. This time, give a more detailed description of each sample.

5. Perform a capillary action experiment on all five samples to test their ability to hold water. The relative amounts of sand, clay, and humus in each sample determine how much water it can hold.

   a. Wet a piece of gauze and attach it to the bottom of a funnel with a rubber band. Repeat this procedure with the other four funnels.

   b. Weigh 50 grams of each soil sample and place the samples in separate funnels. Pack each sample down firmly.

   c. Fill five small flasks with water. Using a graduated cylinder, determine the amount of water in each flask.

   d. Place a funnel in each flask so that the stem of the funnel enters the water.

   e. After 20 minutes, remove the funnels from each flask.

   f. Use the graduated cylinder to measure the amount of water left in each flask.

   g. Record your findings on Data Table 3.

6. Determine the pH of the soil samples using these steps:

   a. Place five pieces of pH paper on a sheet of white paper.

   b. Label the pieces of paper as "CS," "S1," "S2," "S3," and "S4."

   c. Remove the gauze from the funnel with the CS soil and let a drop of the liquid fall on the pH paper, CS.

   d. Repeat this process for the four suspect samples as well.

   e. Record your findings on Data Table 3.

7. Compare samples from Suspects 1 through 4 with the sample from the crime scene and determine if you have a match.

DATA TABLE 1

Initial descriptions.

Sample	Color	Odor	Texture	Plant or animal debris	Inorganic debris present
CS					
S1					
S2					
S3					
S4					

DATA TABLE 2

Observation with microscope.

Sample	Color	Odor	Texture	Plant or animal debris	Inorganic debris present
CS		✕			
S1		✕			
S2		✕			
S3		✕			
S4		✕			

DATA TABLE 3

Water-holding capacity and pH.

Sample	Amount of water held	pH
CS		
S1		
S2		
S3		
S4		

Postlab Questions

1. Did any of the suspects commit the crime? Explain your answer.

_____

_____

_____

2. What is the purpose of the capillary action test?

_____

_____

_____

3. What is soil?

_____

_____

4. Why were the soil samples dried before observations were made?

_____

_____

_____

LESSON 4-6: A DATE WITH THE PAST
A LESSON ON FORENSIC ARCHAEOLOGY

Determining the time when a crime occurred is vital to a criminal investigation. Archaeologists are often used to assist crime scene investigators when a crime occurred in the past.

Detectives of the Past

Field archaeologists are often called "detectives of the past." They use their skills to help unearth evidence, remove it from the ground, and interpret the clues they find. A field archaeologist uses his or her skills to reconstruct the past.

Archaeologists can work with chemists to determine such things as the sex and age of skeletal remains, diseases the victim had suffered in the past, age of victim at death, and the age of the skeletal remains. This information can then be compared to missing person records from long ago to help determine the identity of human remains.

Dating Skeletons

Usually, scientists try to determine the age of human skeletal remains. One method used to date the age of skeletal remains is the Carbon 14 method. Carbon is an element found in all living things. Carbon 14 is an isotope of carbon. Isotopes are atoms with the same number of protons, but different numbers of neutrons.

Carbon 14 dating can be used to find the ages of once-living things because all organisms absorb Carbon 14 when they are alive. Once an organism dies, its body begins to lose Carbon 14 at a fixed rate. Scientists can measure the amount of Carbon 14 remaining in a skeleton to determine the date the person died.

Forensic scientists and archaeologists often form teams to help identify missing persons. They work with complete skeletal remains or small quantities of remains such as bone and tooth fragments. Archaeologists have even been called in to help solve the mystery of individuals murdered in war crimes of the past.

TEACHER NOTES AND KEY FOR LAB 4-6, DATING—RADIOACTIVE STYLE

1. Students need about 50 minutes to complete this activity.

2. This lab is more effective when students use stiff paper, such as posterboard or lightweight cardboard, from which to cut their atoms.

Answers to Data Table

Answers will vary—sample data has been entered.

	Start	*Half life 1—after 10 years*	*Half life 2—after 20 years*	*Half life 3—after 30 years*	*Half life 4—after 40 years*	*Half life 5—after 50 years*	*Half life 6—after 60 years*
Number of atoms that have decayed	0	284	426	497	532	550	559
Number of atoms that remain in sample	567	283	141	70	35	17	8

Answers to Postlab Questions

1. The missing girl was Sue Crayton, reported missing in 1964. Scientists say *90%* of skeletal atoms have decayed. According to our chart, 90% of atoms have decayed after about 30-33 years. 70% remain after 30 years, that is 70/567 = 12% left, so 88% decayed. You know that a little more than 30 years have passed since Sue died, so

$$1998 \quad - \quad 34 \quad = \quad 1964$$

Present date	Years since Sue died	Date of disappearance

Example Line Graph

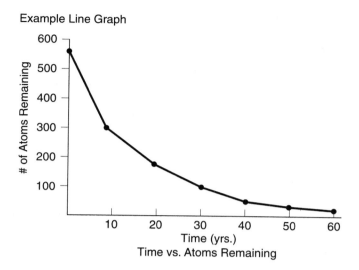

Time vs. Atoms Remaining

2. About 425 atoms; about 13 atoms.

3. Yes. You must have these numbers with which to compare the number of atoms as time passes.

4. They examine skeletal remains and judge the radioactive decay of atoms in those remains.

Name _____ Date _____

DATING—RADIOACTIVE STYLE
A Lab on Forensic Archaeology

Objective

You will use radioactive dating techniques to determine the age of a radioactive material.

Background Information

Stattonville, South Carolina is usually a very quiet community. The year is 1998. Earlier this week some deer hunters stumbled across a suspicious-looking mound of dirt in a heavily wooded area. Crime scene investigators were called in to evaluate the scene.

After determining that this might be a grave, the investigators ask for help from some field archaeologists. Working together, the site is carefully excavated. The skeletal remains of a human are found in the grave.

Citizens state that the area where the skeleton was found has been deserted for about 40 years. The skeletal remains have what appear to be a bullet wound to the skull, so foul play is suspected.

The archaeologists determine that the remains belonged to a female, about age 13. She had been shot at close range through the back of the head. X-rays are taken. Police records turn up missing person reports of ten girls this age. Archaeologists decide to narrow down the range of possibilities by determining how long the young girl has been dead. To do this they must do radioactive dating.

The missing person report looks like this:

Name of girl	Hometown	Date first reported missing
Sue Crayton	Rexty, SC	1964
Brenda Sills	Tebvro, GA	1985
Jane Killow	Loxton, AL	1945
Fay Johnson	Sunville, TN	1935
Mary Sparks	Mayfield, NC	1990
Linda Tims	Brownton, SC	1933
Andrea Brown	Troopville, GA	1985
Jay Sims	Glexton, SC	1900
Kay Thomas	Yexton, AL	1995
Leslie Andrews	Freeport, NC	1920

Your job is to simulate the process of radioactive decay and identify the missing person.

Materials

Shoe box for each group
Stiff white paper (8 × 11-inch)
Scissors
Red crayon
Metric ruler
Graph paper

Procedure, Part A

1. To prepare for this activity, you will make your atoms. Use a red marker to completely color one side of a stiff piece of paper. Place the red side of the paper face down on your desk.

2. On the uncolored side, extending the length of the paper, draw a series of horizontal lines 1 cm apart.

3. Now go back to the top, left edge of the paper and draw a series of vertical lines from top to bottom 1 cm apart until you reach the right edge of the paper. If you have extra edges of the paper left, cut them off and throw them away.

4. Use your scissors to cut out each square you formed in this drawing. You should end up with about 567 squares.

5. Place each of your squares in a shoe box. These squares represent atoms of the radioactive remains taken from the skeleton found in the unmarked grave. These particular atoms have a half life of 10 years.

Procedure, Part B

1. Count the atoms in the box and record this number on the Data Table.

2. Shake the box from side to side to mix your atoms. Dump the atoms on the desk in front of you.

3. Remove all atoms (or squares) that land with their red side up. These atoms have decayed during the first half life (in this case, 10 years). Replace all other atoms to the box. Count the number of atoms you removed. Record this number in the proper location on the Data Table. Subtract from the beginning number to find the number of atoms remaining after half life 1 (10 years).

4. Repeat steps 2 and 3 with the atoms remaining in the box. Record your findings. This will be the number of atoms decayed and the number that remain after the second half life of ten more years. The total decay period now will be 20 years. Remember to subtract the number of the atoms that remain from 567 each time to get the number of atoms that decayed. Each two numbers should add to 567 each time.

5. Repeat the above steps four more times so you will have covered 60 years. Record your findings each time.

© 1998 by The Center for Applied Research in Education

DATA TABLE

	Start	Half life 1—after 10 years	Half life 2—after 20 years	Half life 3—after 30 years	Half life 4—after 40 years	Half life 5—after 50 years	Half life 6—after 60 years
Number of atoms that have decayed	0						
Number of atoms that remain in sample	567						

6. Use your data to make a line graph on which the horizontal axis represents time in years and the vertical axis represents the number of atoms of the radioactive element that remain. Be sure to label your graph.

   Results gathered by the forensic team report that as of this date, the skeletal remains have lost 90% of their radioactive atoms to decay.

Postlab Questions

1. Name the probable missing person. Explain your answer.

   _____

   _____

2. Use your graph to determine how many of the 567 atoms would remain in the sample after about 5 years. How many would you expect to remain in the sample after 55 years?

   _____

3. Was it important to know how many atoms there were in the sample at the start of the experiment? Explain your reason.

   _____

   _____

4. Describe how an archaeologist can help forensic scientists date past crimes.

   _____

   _____

LESSON 4-7: YOUR BONES HAVE A MESSAGE
A LESSON ON FORENSIC ANTHROPOLOGY

Specially trained scientists can identify people by their skeletal remains. If the entire skeleton cannot be located, scientists can use individual bones, bone fragments, and teeth to identify an unfamiliar body. These scientists are called forensic anthropologists.

"Sherlock Bones"

Forensic anthropology was established as a certified science by the FBI in the 1930s. These experts, sometimes jokingly referred to as "Sherlock Bones," regularly use their understanding of the structure and function of the body in their work. Forensic anthropologists prefer to work with complete skeletons, but often only have access to individual bones or teeth. A complete skeleton can reveal a great deal about the once-living individual: physical characteristics, health, lifestyle, habits, injuries, and even cause of death.

When unidentified human bones are located, they are carefully packaged and sent to the laboratory of the forensic anthropologist. These experts attempt to develop a detailed bone and dental record from the remains. Size and shape of certain bones can indicate the age, sex, height, and build of an individual. The condition of the bones can also indicate diseases and general health of the individual at the time of death. The forensic anthropologist carefully examines the bones and records all the information he or she can gather from a visual examination. Then X-rays are used to get a closer look at the condition of the bones.

Head and Hips

The sex of the unknown individual can often be determined by viewing the cranium and pelvic bones. Length of arm and leg bones can be used to calculate the height of the human. Deviations in a bone, such as a lipping at the end of the upper leg bone, indicate that the individual may have been an elderly person with arthritis (inflammation of the joints). Indentations in teeth often indicate the presence of a dental filling at one time. A comparison of the location and shape of these fillings may eventually be matched to the dental records of an individual.

TEACHER NOTES AND KEY FOR LAB 4-7, *MISSING PERSONS*

1. Students need about 50 minutes to complete this lab.

2. Using a black felt-tip pen or marker, trace three copies of Exhibit A onto three large pieces of tracing paper. Paste these to three different pieces of cardboard and tape them in several locations in the room. Students will measure these copies of the exhibit with a metric ruler.

3. If your students have some difficulty working math equations, you may want to do a sample problem with them.

Answers to Crime Scene Report

2. Exhibit A humerus is 25.3 cm in length.

3.

Missing person	Height (feet and inches)	Height (cm)	Calculated length of humerus (cm)
Bill Boston	5′ 11″	180.34	37.958
Jane Caldwell	5′ 5″	165.1	33.555
Ernest Bass	5′ 6″	167.64	33.564
Jill James	4′ 10″	147.32	27.183
Gary Burnes	6′ 10″	208.28	47.626
Lily Walker	5′ 9″	175.26	37.197
Mary Zimmerman	4′ 8″	142.24	25.36
Billy Jenkins	6′ 2″	187.96	40.595
Jessie Agan	6′ 0″	182.88	38.837
Gladys Thomas	5′ 7″	170.18	35.376
Don Harris	5′ 7″	170.18	34.443
Lenny Aires	6′ 4″	193.04	42.353

4. Female
5. Estimated height of owner is 4′ 8″
6. Yes
7. The owner appears to be Mary Zimmerman.
8. Group measurement should mathematically prove that humerus length does indicate height of stature.

Name _____ Date _____

MISSING PERSONS
A Lab on Forensic Anthropology

Objective

You will identify a missing person by using the humerus bone length to find the height of that individual.

Background Information

Last week 12 families received letters from the Federal Bureau of Investigation stating that a human humerus, the upper arm bone, had washed ashore on nearby Seagull Beach. The FBI letter said that it is likely that this upper arm bone belonged to one of 12 missing persons in the area who have never been discovered.

The life insurance policies that covered these 12 individuals have not yet paid the beneficiaries. These polices cannot be paid until proof of the missing person's death has been confirmed. Many of these families are in desperate need of this financial assistance. Most of the familes believe their loved one was murdered.

The length of the upper arm bone can be used to determine the actual height of its owner. For this reason, each of the 12 families has been asked to provide information about the height of their loved one. The members of the crime lab will compare the height of each missing person with the projected height of the individual to whom the humerus belonged. A crime lab report will be sent to the proper insurance company if a match is found for the humerus bone.

Materials

Tape measure (metric)
Calculator
Exhibit A

Procedure

1. Exhibit A is a life-size sketch of the upper arm bone that washed up on Seagull Beach. You and your team of experts will determine the owner of the humerus.

2. Measure the length of the arm bone in centimeters. Record the length of the humerus on your Crime Report Sheet.

© 1998 by The Center for Applied Research in Education

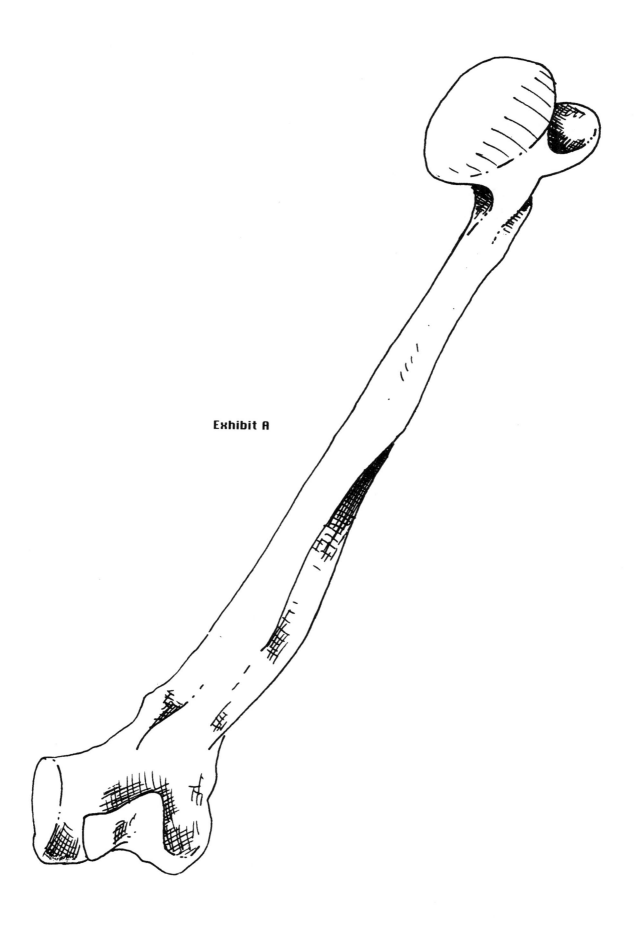

Exhibit A

3. The families of the 12 missing persons have provided information regarding the height of their missing family member to the FBI. Their information is provided on the Data Table. Convert the heights in feet and inches to centimeters. Remember that 2.54 cm equals 1 inch.

4. Use the following formulas to determine whether or not the humerus bone could have belonged to one of these missing persons. Record this information on the Data Table.

   The formula for males and females is different:

   Height of male   = (Length of humerus bone in cm) $\times$ (2.89) + 70.64

   Height of female = (Length of humerus bone in cm) $\times$ (2.79) + 71.48

5. On the Crime Report Sheet indicate the owner of Exhibit A.

Crime Report Sheet

1. Name of Investigators: _____

   Date of Investigation: _____

2. *Results of Investigation:* Length of Exhibit A Humerus: _____ cm

DATA TABLE

3.

Missing person	Height (feet and inches)	Height (cm)	Calculated length of humerus (cm)
Bill Boston	5′ 11″		
Jane Caldwell	5′ 5″		
Ernest Bass	5′ 6″		
Jill James	4′ 10″		
Gary Burnes	6′ 10″		
Lily Walker	5′ 9″		
Mary Zimmerman	4′ 8″		
Billy Jenkins	6′ 2″		
Jessie Agan	6′ 0″		
Gladys Thomas	5′ 7″		
Don Harris	5′ 7″		
Lenny Aires	6′ 4″		

4. Is the owner male or female? _____

5. Estimated height of owner of humerus bone: _____

6. Is one of the 12 missing persons a possible owner? _____

7. Name of probable owner: _____

8. To prove to the insurance company that this formula works, find the height in cm of each person in your investigative team. Then measure the length of each person's humerus. Use your calculations to show that humerus bone length can be used to determine height.